D1357066

The
LITTLE BOOK OF

GREAT
IDEAS

The
LITTLE BOOK OF
GREAT
IDEAS

COMPILED BY

STEPHEN BLAKE
AND
ANDREW JOHN

First published in Great Britain in 2001 by
Michael O'Mara Books Limited
9 Lion Yard
Tremadoc Road
London SW4 7NQ

Copyright © 2001 Michael O'Mara Books Ltd
All rights reserved. No part of this publication may be reproduced, stored
in a retrieval system, or transmitted by any means, without the prior
permission in writing of the publisher, nor be otherwise circulated in any
form of binding or cover other than that in which it is published and
without a similar condition including this condition being imposed on the
subsequent purchaser.

A CIP catalogue record for this book is available from the British Library

ISBN 1-85479-571-6

1 3 5 7 9 10 8 6 4 2

Designed and typeset by Design 23

Printed and bound in Slovenia by Printing House Delo Tiskarna by
arrangement with Korotan Ljubljana.

Contents

Introduction

When we were set the task of coming up with some Great Ideas we didn't know where to start. After all, one person's Great Idea is another person's load of old hogwash.

What's emerged is a little book of stuff – all kinds of stuff: stuff to frazzle your brain when you ponder on whether or not you actually exist; stuff about how people on trains would be bereft of mobile phones were it not for the Industrial Revolution; stuff about gods; stuff about skateboards and hula hoops; stuff about computers and stuff about all sorts of stuff … Oh, oodles of stuff. And some stuff and nonsense.

You won't pass your GCSEs, your highers or your baccalaureates by reading this book (although you might get a PhD from one of the new universities). What you will get, though, are a lot of facts and, we hope, a few giggles.

We haven't covered all the Great Ideas – there are just so many of them. But we've had some fun with a few of them (and been just a tad more serious with others), whether they're actual, tangible things such as inventions or the more abstract ideas such as schools of philosophy or art. And we've presented them in no particular order because it's more fun that way (although we've helped you out by making some words bold if they refer to something else in the book).

Many Great Ideas come in the world of technology, of course, and these advances, perhaps more than anything, have shaped our lives and culture in such profound ways. But there are many Greats to be found in the world of ideas itself – philosophy – some in areas you can't really categorize, and others that many people won't consider Great Ideas at all, such as silly crazes. Most do come under technology and philosophy, though, as reflected by how big those sections are in this little book.

But all of them will be considered great by somebody – even if it's only us.

OK. That's all. Briefing over. Read on, Macduff.

Stephen Blake and Andrew John – June 2001

Passions and Crazes

In the UK we pride ourselves on being a bit crazy, but we tend to prefer the word 'eccentric' – far more civilized, some say.

We must be a few balls short of an over to have come up with cricket, after all! And there are a number of others that have begun life in the UK, and some that haven't. Here are some of the best of them.

•

The hula hoop Welcome to the wonderful world of hip injuries. In the 1950s and 1960s people could be seen with colourful bands of plastic being gyrated around their midriffs in an effort to reduce the size of said midriffs. At the time, this was called Fun. Looking back on it from the 2000s, we wonder why its practitioners weren't considered to be not in full possession of their faculties!

The term 'hula hoop' came about because of the resemblance to the Hawaiian hula dance, whose movements could be vaguely discerned in the more proficient hula-hoop practitioners who hadn't toppled over.

These plastic circles, usually about a metre (3 feet) in diameter, would be placed over the body, held against the waist and then set in an eccentric motion, using the human body as an axis of gyration, as the pelvis was swung around in a circular motion in order to keep the hoop going. Still with us?

What usually happened was that, as the practitioner of this bizarre form of exercise became tired, uncoordinated or just a bit fed up with the exercise, the hula hoop would gradually find its way to the floor. Participants would then laugh uproariously. Or the violent lurching of the pelvis in order to get the thing started constituted such a trauma to the skeleton that some participants of a certain age would collapse amid the noise of cracking bones. The laughter was then a little more subdued and usually behind hands.

To get over this problem, we've invented the Motorized Hula Hoop™ (pat. pending), which means you can just stand and let it do its stuff. In fact, we highly recommend adding a shop-window dummy and letting the Motorized Hula Hoop™ do its stuff on that while you go out and have some steak and chips.

This practice of swinging the hips just to get the hoop gyrating around your waist, by the way, was known to happen in civilized countries. Why it largely died out is anybody's guess – but when the Sixties came along, well, that era brought all sorts of strange behaviour to take people's minds off such things as hula hoops.

●

The Frisbee Another craze that came in the 1950s, this involves throwing a concave, platter-like disc with a flick of the wrist, and watching it fly aimlessly, if gracefully, through the air, thereby necessitating an otherwise needless journey to go and pick it up – assuming it hasn't alighted halfway up a tree or in the middle of a lake. If you can train your dog to fetch it, OK, but the chew marks around the edges soon compromise the disc's aerodynamic qualities, causing the thing to return like a boomerang and deal you a sudden and unexpected injury to the head, leaving you convinced that the dog is having a laugh at your expense.

In the United States, the World Flying Disc Federation holds championships in the throwing of this device. But they probably have other people to catch the things.

The razor-edged metal version of the Frisbee could, we submit, be used to make public beheadings more interesting in certain countries whose practices the West likes to turn a blind eye to. Please don't try this at home.

•

The micro-scooter A Great Idea for nipping around and dodging traffic jams – but, as with most things you enjoy, unsafe in some circumstances, and probably illegal in others. The Great part is that they're small and light and easily transportable.

However, look at this statistic: '... 2,200 people in the UK were involved in accidents involving children's scooters…' What we've missed off that quotation – from Roger Vincent, of the Royal Society of the Prevention of Accidents, which appeared in a September 2000 edition of the Guardian – is its first two words, 'In 1998 …' That was before the micro-scooter craze took off – and that's only in the UK.

It's not just kids who use these nifty little modes of transport: adults do, too. As far as UK law is concerned, oddly enough, whether they're strictly legal is open to question. They shouldn't be ridden on the road – that goes against the law (as far as we know) and against common sense, because of the obvious dangers – and shouldn't be ridden on pavements. They probably come under the same 1835 Highways Act that prevents bicycles from being ridden on pavements – not that anybody pays attention to that. Some safety experts even advise the wearing of helmets and knee and elbow pads.

The micro-scooter is made of aircraft-grade aluminium, hence its lightness, but is otherwise similar in shape to the older push-scooters. It folds, so you can tuck it into a wallet or handbag. Well, you can try.

It was devised by Wim Ouboter, a Swiss inventor, and appeared on the market in 1998 – but such was the demand that production couldn't keep up, and a host of imitation brands popped up. Some manufacturers weren't too fussy about safety and one British trading standards expert, Brian Croft of Liverpool, complained that many were coming in from China and Taiwan – and British law didn't require manufacturers to tell authorities in Britain how the scooters were tested.

•

The yo-yo The yo-yo has been found in the capacious pockets of various Doctors (note the capital 'D' – we're talking serious cult sci-fi here), because this eccentric character is as fond of this little toy as he is of old-fashioned London police boxes.

It's been around in Europe and America since the 1930s, having originated in the Philippine Islands. Basically, a length of string is secured to and wrapped around the central spindle of a small spool. One end of the string is held in the hand, usually with the help of a small loop around the middle finger, and the spool is let go, spinning as its own weight causes the string to unwind from the spindle part, then springing back as it changes rotational direction when the string runs out, gathering the string up again as it returns to its owner's hand. But you probably knew all that already!

•

The Beatles There's our old friend from Mars, right, and he comes to Earth and hears a news story on the BBC, uttered in authoritative tones by a Radio 4 newsreader, concerning an ex-beetle called George Harrison (this was after he had been in the news in 2000 and 2001). Talk of an ex-beetle must have sounded odd indeed.

But everyone has heard of The Beatles, of course. Were they a Great Idea? History seems to think so – and so did (and do) the so-called Fab Four's millions of fans worldwide.

This soaraway phenomenon comprised John Lennon (1940–80), Paul McCartney (b. 1942),

George Harrison (b. 1943) and Ringo Starr (Richard Starkey, b. 1940), and came together in 1960. The songwriting pair in the foursome were Lennon and McCartney, who had met at a fête in 1957, while Lennon was still with a skiffle band called The Quarry Men, which he'd formed a year before, after his Aunt Mimi had bought him a guitar. The Quarry Men made their first appearance at the famous Cavern Club in Liverpool in August 1957. Unhappily, Paul (now Sir Paul) McCartney was not able to be with them as he was away at Scout Camp. George

Harrison joined in 1958.

The band became The Beatles in 1960, with Stuart Sutcliffe as bass player. He left the group in 1961 and Paul McCartney took over bass. Initially, The Beatles' drummer was Pete Best, but he was sacked and Ringo Starr joined in 1962.

The Beatles' music began as rock and roll, but over the next ten years other influences – Indian music, chamber music, electronic music – were to be found in their copious output. Most of their music was characterized by melodious tunes and innovative chord sequences, and their lyrics touched the conscience of any who cared to listen. And many did.

Their music is still issued, and other bands continue to emulate their sound. And what a sound! Lennon and McCartney have gone down in history as two of the most innovative songwriters of the pop era – innovative not only in their lyrics but in their chord sequences, too. Small wonder, perhaps, that many parents of a more old-fashioned persuasion thought it odd that their offspring should be so enraptured by four young men with mop-head hair styles and (it seemed at the time) a pretty weird mode of attire.

But were they, as many have speculated, the Great Idea of one Brian Epstein? Certainly, he seemed to have a big hand in turning them into something commercially viable, after he'd seen them play a concert and decided he wanted to be their manager. He encouraged them to dress more neatly and got a deal for them with Parlaphone in July 1962 – two months before Ringo's arrival.

Well, after their debut single, 'Love Me Do', in October 1962, which reached number 17 in the charts, it was all plain sailing: successful albums, chart-topping singles, tours.

They became successful in the States after an appearance on *The Ed Sullivan Show* in February 1964. An estimated 73 million people saw that – more than the entire population of the UK.

Films followed: *A Hard Day's Night* (1964), *Help!* (1965).

In August 1966, at Candlestick Park, San Francisco, The Beatles performed their last concert, and retreated to the studio. In 1967 they released the trademark 'Penny Lane'/ 'Strawberry Fields Forever' single, and the album 'Sergeant Pepper's Lonely Hearts Club Band' emerged in that same year. (Useless Information Department: that album took more than 700 hours of studio time and used orchestra, brass band and psychedelic music.)

Although there was further output in the following years, band members were actually collaborating less frequently, and they split in April 1970.

John Lennon was assassinated by a gunman in New York on 8 December 1980. That might have been the end of Beatles music, but in 1995 a single, 'Free as a Bird', based on a 1977 demo recording by Lennon, to which other members of the band had added new tracks, was released.

A series of albums followed. In 2000, 'One' was released, being an album of The Beatles' Number One singles.

•

The game of cricket In Britain they take it for granted: it's a very British thing. There's even a saying for something that's deemed unfair: 'I say: that's just not cricket!'

We have to go back to the middle of the sixteenth century to see the first evidence of this barmy ballgame. And the first recorded match between two English counties came in 1709, when Kent took on Surrey. They don't have rules in cricket: they have laws. The first set of these came about in 1744.

And, while you may think women's cricket is a modern phenomenon, it actually began in 1745 in Guildford, where it's thought the game itself began, although it was called 'creckett' then. But it was not to be until 1976 that the first women's test match was held at Lord's cricket ground in London, although a test between England and Australia was held in Brisbane in 1934.

The laws of cricket are made and published by the Marylebone Cricket Club, or the MCC,

which was set up in 1787. About two and a half centuries after our game of 'creckett' in

Guildford, the Australians cottoned onto the idea that belting a ball with a stick and running up and down 22 yards of wicket was a Great Idea. The game was introduced there in 1803.

The first international match recorded didn't involve England – it was between the USA and Canada in 1844.

Limited-overs cricket is a fairly new thing (and must have seemed like sacrilege to the die-hards of the longer game), and the first international match played to these laws was between England and Australia in Melbourne in 1971.

What makes cricket so eccentric in the eyes of non-cricketing nations is that a match can go on for anything between a day and … well, try this for a statistic: in the final test of England's 1938–39 tour of South Africa, the game started on 3 March and was abandoned, without a result, eleven days later!

Then there's this thing called the Ashes (note the capital 'A'). These are the ashes of a bail, burned in Australia in the middle of the nineteenth century. The Ashes have an interesting history. In 1882, Australia beat England on England's own turf at the Oval, and a sporting paper published a spoof funeral notice, saying that the body would be cremated and the ashes would be taken to Australia. But an England cricket captain, Ivo Bligh, promised he'd bring back 'those Ashes'. When his team actually won – in Australia – some Melbourne women are said to have burned a bail and presented them to Bligh in a small urn. That urn of ashes remains at Lord's cricket ground, home of the MCC, no matter who wins them. So it's ironic, since England hasn't won the Ashes for goodness knows how long, that it always has custody of them, but the winner of the Ashes series is said to 'hold' the Ashes.

The first bowler to take 500 wickets – which happened on 19 March 2001 – was the West Indian player Courtney Walsh during the West Indies' game in Trinidad against South Africa, bringing congratulations not only from his teammates, but also from the West Indies prime minister, P. J. Patterson.

Of all sports, cricket seems to epitomize relaxed summer days, and has a romantic quality with the proverbial thwack of leather against willow and the ripples of polite applause from the stands. While it has become a big spectator sport played by professionals (that wasn't always so, and, indeed, amateurs were deemed to be superior when professionals entered the game), it will be a long time before that romantic image disappears completely from people's memories.

•

The boomerang The returning version of this little gadget was invented by dentists, so that they'd get all the business of cleaning up the mouths of people who'd stood hypnotized by the aerodynamics of the thing until it had come back and given them a nasty crack on the jaw!

Well, that's our theory, anyway.

What we do know is that it's used by Australian Aborigines both for sport and as a weapon – and it can pack a punch.

There are two types. There are probably more, but we're not doing minutiae here, OK? So, there are two main types: returning and non-returning. The first returns to you and the second, like the Frisbee, doesn't, and you have to go and fetch it, putting you at great risk of being hit by someone else's boomerang.

Boomerangs are usually made of wood, and are roughly V-shaped, with slightly skewed arms. The arms are sharpened, but one surface is flat and the other is convex. This is part of what gives them their aerodynamic qualities.

The return boomerang is used for hunting small birds, as well as for sport. It's thrown vertically, but inclines to its flat side and then curves and obediently returns to the thrower. (Inexperienced throwers should not try this in the bedroom or lounge.)

The non-returning boomerang is usually bigger and heavier and is used for hunting large game. And it can pack a mighty blow from a distance of about 150 metres (500 feet).

While the boomerang is associated mostly with Australian Aborigines, it's also used by the Hopi people of Arizona, and peoples of southern India and north-eastern Africa.

•

The skateboard Who could be so insensitive as to put the words 'daffy' and 'shooting the duck' into the same context? But this has nothing to do with cute cartoon characters: they are two of the techniques used in this crazy pastime that has pedestrians running into shop doorways to avoid the possibility of a nasty collision and spilled shopping!

Because these modes of transport are a bit like short surfboards, the activity has sometimes been called 'land surfing' or 'skurfing'. It began in California about 1960, when surfers couldn't always find somewhere to do their thing, so some bright spark came up with the idea of attaching a short surfboard to roller skates.

It wasn't long, of course – entrepreneurialism being what it is in the States – before someone purpose-built these things and called them skateboards.

By 1965 there was even a movie, *Skater-Dater*, which made the craze even more popular, and by the end of the 1970s it was all around the world. The first official world championships were held in California in 1977. The craze started to weaken in the eighties and had waned even more by the early nineties, but has since seen a revival of interest..

But let's end where we came in: as well as the daffy and shooting the duck, there are many other manoeuvres, including the space walk, the helicopter, the kick turn, the wheelie, the power slide, the kick flip, the bunny hop, tic-tacking, the endover, walking the dog and barrel jumping.

•

Diana, Princess of Wales How the UK – and, indeed, the world – mourned when Diana, Princess of Wales met her tragic and untimely death – or indulged in a display of questionable sentiment, according to your point of view.

Diana Frances Spencer (1961–97) was actually born in a rented house – but it was on a royal estate, at Sandringham.

When she was young, she used to play with the younger sons of Queen Elizabeth II, brothers of the heir to the throne, Charles, Prince of Wales. After a spell at a finishing school in Switzerland, Diana shared a house in Kensington with three other women, and worked as a kindergarten teacher.

On 24 February 1981, she and Charles announced that they were to be married – and married they were, causing widespread disruption to traffic and many favourite TV programmes that were re-scheduled or cancelled. Diana gave birth to their sons William and Harry in 1982 and 1984 respectively.

But Diana was more than just a Queen-to-be: she was made into a Great Idea by the media – especially when her marriage began to show signs of strain. Known as the People's Princess, she was a great Doer of Good Works, and helped charities galore by lending her name and her patronage.

The Prince and Princess of Wales were divorced on 28 August 1996, but Diana retained her title. She continued her charity work, although scaled it down so that she could enjoy more privacy, for no one, it seemed, had ever before been so hotly pursued by the British media. The tabloids stalked her with unrelenting zeal, displaying their usual hunger for stories about royalty and celebrities.

On 31 August 1997, the nation awoke to the news that Diana was dead, killed in a car crash in Paris, prompting dozens of conspiracy theories to rival those that followed the assassination of JFK. There is now a Diana Memorial Fund to help those causes she was most fond of.

Technology and Other Cleverness

However could we manage without technology? Well, perhaps that's a pointless question, really, because we didn't know it was coming along! But, come on, admit that you'd rather be without your gadgets and gizmos, computers and calculators, TVs and toasters, microlights and microwaves and all the other handy little alliterative pairs you can come up with. Admit that you'd rather go back to nature and grow your own food, gather water from the stream or communal well, crochet your own couscous.

Or maybe not. The fact is, technology's been with us – in varying degrees, of course – since someone invented the wheel. And look what that led to.

So, lest we get carried away, let the words of the Swiss dramatist Max Frisch (1911–91), bring us back to earth: he said technology was 'the knack of so arranging the world that we need not experience it'.

•

The wheel Bet you've never really thought just how useless this thing is. Go on, have a think. What can you do with a wheel? On its

own. Not attached to anything. Just a wheel.

You can roll it down a hill. That could be fun for a while, until you get that sudden urge to watch paint dry. You could make it out of light plastic and use it as a hula hoop. But there's not much else. In fact, it was probably around for centuries, languishing in a caveman's garage or potting shed, while he pondered on what to do with it, hoping someone, somewhere, would invent the double-decker bus so he could put his invention to good use.

And yet the wheel was the first-ever piece of technological wizardry. Build that double-decker bus or a roller skate on top of a few of them and you've got mobility. Build a clock around them and you can tell the time. Add them to a machine and all manner of things are possible.

Imagine life without it: no cars, no gears, no clock movements, no waterwheels, flywheels, paddle wheels, pulley wheels, no Catherine wheels, no prayer wheels, no London Eye.

It's hard to think of anything technological

that doesn't involve wheels. We tend to think mainly of vehicle wheels, but the wheel has been responsible for much more than that – and, indeed, the potter's wheel was around before wheels were used for land transport, which is thought to be around 5,500 to 6,000 years ago. The first use of a wheel could have been the quern, a device made of two circular stones and used for grinding grain.

The earliest evidence we have of a wheeled vehicle is from the Tigris–Euphrates valley dating from around 3000 BC. Early wheels were solid affairs, made either of one piece of wood or a number of planks, but spoked wheels came into the picture as early as 2000 BC, and evidence has been found in places as far apart as China, Mesopotamia and Scandinavia.

Spokes themselves aren't the simple, decorative things that seem to make wheels look nicer: indeed, the chap who produced the 'ordinary' (see **The bicycle**), James Starley, invented 'tangential spoking' (these days a tangential spokesman is known as a spin doctor), which was an arrangement whereby the spoke ran from hub to circumference in a crossover pattern, giving added strength.

Wheels on today's vehicles are mostly made of pressed steel or cast aluminium. And they're still round.

•

The clock The time you really notice how many clocks you have in your home is when it's time to change to or from British Summer Time or daylight saving. That's when you start to curse them.

You spend half an hour changing your bedside timepiece, the one on the wall in the kitchen, the one on the mantelpiece in the lounge, the one in your electronic diary, the one on your wrist, the one in the car, the one on the fax machine, the one on the video, the one on the electronic time switch that turns appliances on and off, the one that controls the immersion heater … Then you forget just one of them – and that's the one vital to your day's timetable. The only one you don't have to worry about – usually, anyway – is the one on your computer: it usually adjusts on first boot-up after the clocks have changed.

Weren't we better off without them? In the days when we burned a piece of rope and noted how long it took to burn from knot to knot? In

the days when we stuck a stick in the ground and studied the movement of the shadow?

Indeed, it's the shadow variety that preceded the clock, and an Egyptian shadow clock of the eighth century is still in existence. Along came the sundial, of which Hilaire Belloc (1870–1953) wrote:

I am a sundial, and I make a botch
Of what is done much better by a watch.

So clocks, on reflection, are probably a Great Idea after all. The origin of the mechanical clock is obscure, but thought to date from the fourteenth century. It wasn't called a clock then, but 'horologium'. Top marks to the person who invented the word 'clock' – it's a lot easier to say.

'Clock' originally meant bell, and got its name from the huge mechanical time indicators in medieval bell towers. They were cumbersome devices that needed weights to drive them. Then came the pendulum. A Dutch physicist called Christiaan Huygens (1629–95) demonstrated in 1657 how to use a pendulum to run a clock.

Robert Hooke (1635–1703), an English physicist, improved on this ten years later by devising an escapement within the timepiece that allowed for pendulums with a shorter arc of oscillation.

Clocks are often not just time-tellers, but decoration, too, and the cuckoo clock was made in the Black Forest of Germany as far back as 1730. There have been clocks shaped like bird cages, grandfather (or case) clocks, with the pendulum mechanism showing beneath the other workings and, no doubt, many other weird and not so wonderful shapes and sizes.

Mass production of the clock can be traced to the USA after the War of Independence – but a dearth of metal meant that wood was used for the moving parts. It had to be highly seasoned, of course. The USA soon became the biggest mass-producer of clocks in the world.

So it's not surprising that an American, Henry E. Warren, invented the electric clock – in the early 1900s. He persuaded electricity companies to time the cycles of alternating current in such a way that synchronous motors could be used to drive clocks.

The quartz clock we're more familiar with today was an American invention, too, but it may surprise you to know that it's been around since 1929 – and an improvement on that was the caesium atomic clock made in the UK in 1955. You may not believe this when you're constantly adjusting your quartz-controlled wristwatch, but with the better-quality devices, the maximum error is one second per ten years.

If you want real accuracy – and, let's face it, nobody outside a laboratory really does – then you need your very own atomic clock. These rely for their precision on oscillation frequencies between two energy states of certain atoms or molecules. A caesium-atom clock is used to define time within the *Système International d'Unités* (SI for short). The frequency of the energy absorbed by a caesium atom as it changes from a lower to a higher energy level is measured, and this defines time. Since that process can't be affected by external forces, you can guarantee no niggling little bug or gust of wind will knock time as we know if off course and result in burned dinners and missed appointments all over the world.

But it would make life interesting.

•

DNA fingerprinting This must count as one of the greatest contributions to modern forensic science. Deoxyribonucleic acid (DNA) contains the so-called building blocks of our very being, and is found in the double helix of molecules found in the nuclei of our cells.

The complete DNA of each individual is unique (except in the case of identical twins), so a DNA sample taken from blood, hair or a piece of skin or saliva and matched with DNA found at the scene of a crime is pretty good evidence of culpability, even though, in some scientific circles, DNA's uniqueness to an individual has been brought into question.

It's sometimes called DNA typing, and it was developed in the mid-eighties initially for medical purposes, to enable experts to detect inherited diseases. The first time it was used in a criminal investigation in the UK was in 1987.

The reason the accuracy of DNA testing has been challenged is that only a segment, and not the entire DNA, is examined. If an individual segment of the DNA could conceivably be the same in several human beings, is there not the theoretical chance that a mismatch could be made? Then there's the human factor, leaving room for error.

Another objection is cost. Because it's so expensive, a suspect may not be able to afford his or her own DNA tests to try to refute forensic evidence.

There's been a lot of controversy in the UK over insurance companies who want to study people's genetic profiles to see if they're predisposed to particular illnesses. It is alleged that insurers could then hike up their premiums or refuse to insure them.

•

The widget This handy little device gets stones out of horses' hooves, fits snugly into all machines to ensure the correct flibbeting of the gronge sprocket, reverses the polarity of the neutron flow in all but the most basic design of pantyhose, cleans toenails and bath plugs, removes blackheads and lets you seem to be going when you're coming back.

In short, it's a nonsense – a humorously euphonious word that can be used for just about any gadget, gizmo, thingummy or thingamajig you like. No technical dictionary would be complete without a reference to it; no laboratory or workshop should be without one.

Some manufacturers of canned beer went and ruined it all, though, by putting a little device into their cans that produced a creamy head on the beer. They called it … yes, a widget. And that rather spoiled things, because we tend to like handy, meaningless little words that you can use when you can't think of the one that's on the tip of your tongue.

Perhaps someone will think of another word that sounds just as endearing.

•

Printing The good thing about this Great Idea is that it's so well documented – it has to be.

Printing goes back further than we thought. Further than *we* thought – *you* may be an expert on the subject and know all about it! It goes back, in fact, to ancient Babylonian times, and the use of signet stones. These were used to make impressions in clay, either as a signature or a religious symbol.

Printing processes developed at different times, independently of one another in many cases, in different parts of the world. Although

not strictly printing as we know it, books in the early Egyptian, Greek and Roman civilizations were laboriously written out by scribes, time and time again. Books were also produced in medieval monasteries.

But where printing really took off was with the invention of movable type. This concept arose in tenth-century China, but, because the

Chinese language has thousands of separate characters, it didn't catch on all that well. The Koreans invented movable type made from moulds in the fourteenth century, but they, too, found it not too practical, and preferred printing from blocks, which had preceded it.

It wasn't until the fifteenth century that movable type was first used in Europe, a development that was unrelated to earlier ones in the Far East. There were huge differences, too. Inks were different – oil-based from the start – and individual letters were held together by pressure applied at either end of the line on the tray that held the type. The Eastern printers had used water-based inks, and their type was often held together with clay.

Coinciding with this development in the mid-fifteenth century was the availability of paper in abundance. And the growing number of literate middle-class people were demanding quality reading matter.

Johann Gutenberg (c. 1400–68), of Mainz in

Germany is frequently credited with the invention of printing. But historians in other countries, notably the Netherlands and France, have produced evidence to show that printing was invented in their own countries.

The real power of print, of course, is that knowledge could be spread. And that led to censorship – especially, in those times, by the church. Such censorship was introduced in 1487 by Pope Innocent VIII, and printers had to submit work to church authorities before it could be published.

One of the duties of the Congregation of the Holy Office – or the Universal Roman Inquisition, as it was known – was that of censorship.

A similar system was set up in England by Henry VIII, who made printers submit their manuscripts to church authorities for vetting.

Pamphleteering was one of the most popular uses of printing, and pamphlets were widely circulated in the sixteenth and seventeenth centuries, full of religious and political propaganda.

The first printing presses were based on those used by farmers to make olive oil. They were crude compared with today's far more sophisticated presses, and consisted of a device for pressing the paper onto the type using a screw mechanism. A surface called a platen held the paper against the type.

It was slow and cumbersome, with only about 250 impressions per hour possible – on one side of the paper at a time, of course. Eventually levers and springs replaced the screw mechanism.

So far, presses had been made of wood, but

began to be made of iron around 1800. Because bigger forms could be used (a form is the frame that holds the type), bigger sheets of printed paper could be produced.

The press most of us are familiar with is the rotary press, which was a nineteenth-century development. One of these was known as the 'perfecting press', which printed on both sides of the paper at the same time. But presses were still printing on sheets. In 1863 an American inventor, William A. Bullock, patented a press that allowed paper to be fed from rolls, and in 1871 the continuous-roll press was perfected by another American, a printer called Richard March Hoe, which could run off 18,000 newspapers in an hour.

Computers control modern printing presses, adjusting for colour density and a whole host of other variables. But before computers moved in on the act, it would be a machine-room manager or another seasoned printer who would take samples of the output and cast an expert eye over it for fluctuations in quality.

It's odd that, in the days of the computer and information technology, we use words such as 'font' and 'typeface' while our work is still in the form of pixels on a screen and before it has found its way on to anything as solid as paper.

•

The computer Once upon a time we were happy totting up a row of figures, handwriting a letter or looking up something in an encyclopedia made of paper and, if it took half an hour, well, so be it.

Nowadays, if you have to wait as long as fifteen seconds for your computer to connect to the Internet or load a program, you're drumming your fingers with impatience and probably mumbling oaths directed at Mr Babbage under your breath .

For Charles Babbage (1792–1871) it was who designed mechanical gizmos that anticipated the modern computer – that instrument on most of our desks that we now think we can't do without.

Babbage, a Devon-born mathematician and inventor, began to amuse himself with a gadget called a 'difference engine' in the 1820s – something that took up most of his life. It was initially built to compile logarithm tables – and even anticipated the colour desktop colour printers sitting alongside your tower CPU, because it was designed to print stuff out, using different colours and typefaces to make the results easier to read.

Mr Babbage never got to finish his life's work, however, because of lack of funding, and the challenge was taken on by other scientists after his death.

But there were other precursors to the digital computer we've come to know and love/hate. Blaise Pascal (1623–1662), the French philosopher, physicist and mathematician, devised the first adding machine in 1642. And it had teeth. There were ten of them on each of ten wheels. The teeth represented the digits 0 to 9. By advancing the wheels a given number of teeth, it was possible to add numbers to one another.

As you would expect, several people came along and improved on this, including Gottfried Wilhelm Leibniz (1646–1716), the German mathematician, philosopher and statesman, who went forth and devised a machine that could also multiply.

Herman Hollerith (1860–1929), an American statistician, discovered in the 1880s a means of using punched cards (some people remember those as being in use in recent decades, of course, such has been the speed of technological change). And this brings us back to Mr Babbage, for, as well as his difference engine, he also devised the 'analytical engine', which used those punched cards as a store for saving data. While this is not the sort of book to go into the minutiae of scientific principles, we can be sure that it was, indeed, a Great Idea. And this, along with the amazing Mr Babbage's difference engine, was a precursor to the modern computer.

Again, Babbage failed to put his invention into practice, although it was probably possible, technically speaking, to do so at that time.

And so we come through early-twentieth-century analogue computers using their rotating shafts of gears, through electrical versions, to the first electronic computer, which was called Colossus and was devised by a team of scientists working during World War II at Bletchley Park in the South of England. Colossus incorporated 1,500 vacuum tubes.

That frightfully clever man Alan Turing (1912–54) headed the team that used this machine to crack the notorious Enigma code.

Well, a lot has happened since then. The transistor, for instance, was introduced into computers in the late fifties, and speeded things up a bit, as well as using less power and having a longer life than vacuum tubes. So they gave rise to what was known as the second generation of computers. The integrated circuit (IC) came in during the late sixties, allowing far more versatility because many transistors could be incorporated on one substrate of silicon.

Large-scale integrated circuits (LSIs) were introduced in the seventies, followed by very large-scale integrated circuits (VLSIs), and with them the microprocessor, allowing thousands of interconnected transistors.

Well, to cut a long story short, modern computers are all conceptually similar. Add input devices such as keyboards, mice, light pens and scanners, and output devices such as printers, and you have today's mind-blowing computer systems. These are often to be found sitting on a child's desk, said child probably knowing more about their operation than parent or guardian, and having to teach said parent or guardian how to set up the very controls that prevent objectionable material coming down from the Internet that's not suitable for said child to see!

The Internet There was a time when 'surfing' meant standing on a board and riding a wave. Now we 'surf' this phenomenon called the Internet – or at least the websites that it has made possible. And everywhere you turn, it seems, words such as 'web', 'the Net' and 'download' are being written and spoken by people of all ages.

But, despite all the seamier stuff that can come down the lines from websites the world over – and some material that is, let's face it, plain boring – the Internet is another Great Idea.

The thing about the Internet is that it's organic: as more and more people set up more and more websites, without reference to some central authority or digital holding centre for information, it just keeps on growing.

The Internet is so much taken for granted now that we're apt to forget that there was once a world without it. And, when we do think about it, we tend to see the Net as a very recent phenomenon. Well, in its present form, it is. But you may be surprised to know that it goes back to the early 1970s – 1973, to be exact – when the technology to drive it was created by Vincent Cerf as part of a US Department of Defense project. The project and the technology were handed over to the private sector and government scientific agencies in 1984 for further development.

The rest, as they say, is history, and by 2000 you could access the Net from more than 200 countries. Now we can surf the World Wide Web (a network of websites) and we can buy books, records and a host of other goods from trading sites, we can download pictures and graphics, we can visit websites for research purposes, and of course we can have fun just browsing.

•

The biro There are still people who insist on using a fountain pen, of course, disliking the inky paste that rolls out over the ball of a ballpoint pen. But the biro h  now become so much a par of our lives that it has a lowercase 'b' – the word has become assimilated, the way 'hoover' is used for a vacuum cleaner (even if it's not actually made by Hoover!), and as a verb, too, for the act of using one.

The idea of the biro – or ballpoint pen – had been tinkered with during the nineteenth century (although they didn't call it a biro then). But getting the right type of ink presented a few problems: the writing would have gaps in it where the pen skipped, and the ink was slow to dry, making it susceptible to smudging.

It was not until 1938 that a Hungarian inventor called Georg Biro created an oil-based ink that was just the job. Mind you, when a biro leaks in your pocket you certainly know about it!

Now we have biros that write in many

colours – some, indeed, have several refills in the one body, and you select which colour you want. And there are even ballpoint pens of sorts – the rollerball variety – whose writing is as smooth as that of a fountain pen! Seems like the best of both worlds, especially as one thing a fountain pen can't do is write with enough pressure to go through a wad of carbon copies over half an inch thick.

•

The battery Without this handy little device we wouldn't have the mobile phone, the personal stereo, the electric toothbrush and dozens of other terribly useful gadgets and gizmos. And some would say 'amen' to that.

It probably seems a bit mind-boggling to think of actual electricity – that dynamic power that drives so much in our lives – stored in a static, if somewhat heavy, box or cylinder. But a battery is a way of converting energy stored in chemicals into electrical energy. Simple, really.

One major breakthrough in storage of electricity was with the lead acid battery, which was invented in 1859 by Gaston Planté, and which could be recharged.

This battery is still used in cars and other forms of transport, and is made up of a group of cells connected together in series. Each cell has a lead plate, a lead oxide plate and an electrolytic solution of sulphuric acid. It's recharged by the forcing of a current through the battery in the opposite direction to the one the current flows in when the battery is charged.

Nickel metal hydride, zinc-chlorine and sodium sulphur batteries are among the most modern, and show some promise for possible use in electric vehicles. So far they have been limited in the distance they can be expected to run on one single charge of the battery, but it can't be long before battery technology brings us quieter (and less poisonous) modes of transport.

•

The spinning jenny Actually, the jenny was only part – but an important part – of the process of creating our clothes and other fabrics. Without the spinning process, we'd still be wearing fig leaves – although where you get a good supply of those in colder countries is anybody's guess.

Jenny was the daughter of James Hargreaves (1720–78), who is credited with the invention of the spinning machine that bears her name. It

made the automatic production of cotton thread possible, by simulating the actions of a spindle and distaff, and produced yarns of similar character.

Richard Arkwright (1732–92) came along, took Hargreaves's principle and turned it into a water-powered machine that enabled home spinning to take on industrial proportions.

Enter Samuel Crompton (1753–1827), who invented the mule (not the four-legged variety). This could make yarn so quickly that a surplus was created in England. Then came another inventor called Edmund Cartwright (1743–1823), who during the 1780s applied power to the loom and revolutionized the conversion of yarns into cloth. Very soon the use of a simple spinning wheel at home was a dying craft.

The mechanized production of textiles was one factor in the Industrial Revolution.

•

The Industrial Revolution Some argue that this was not a Great Idea – that we were better off as an agrarian society. Like all revolutionary ideas, though, advances in technology are neither good nor bad in themselves but, the way we use them can be.

It's hard to pinpoint just where the Industrial Revolution began (so it was not really one Great Idea, but many that just happened to coalesce into a social and industrial phenomenon), but it involved advances in a number of areas, including textiles and steam power, giving rise to the factory system, setting up the conflicting relationship between workers and the factory-owning capitalists, of whom Marx had much to say.

Although the Industrial Revolution began in Britain, its effects were soon felt worldwide. Britain started it all because of its huge trading links and its empire, greatly facilitating the import of such items as cotton. Soon, there was mass migration to the cities and away from the hitherto agrarian way of life.

Another development was the invention in the eighteenth century of an efficient form of steam engine by James Watt, and the process of iron smelting was considerably advanced by James Darby, and there soon followed the blast furnace of James Smeaton.

Flying shuttles, spinning jennys and mules all helped to revolutionize the textile industry, and, before you knew it, we had child labour, cramped and unhealthy cities, industrial disputes and appalling working conditions.

At the end of the nineteenth century, electricity largely took over from steam power, new methods of working were introduced, including the division of labour to maximize factory output, and a network of canals, and eventually railways, improved transportation.

Soon, as the Industrial Revolution spread, politics, power structures and economies were being changed worldwide, and life would never be the same again.

The World Wide Web Or www for short – but it takes longer to say.

This is something else that, like the Internet, we tend to think has been around for ever. Certainly, it's a big part of the lives of so many of us now that we can be excused for wondering how we managed without it.

You can get just about everything these days from one website or another, and have a lot of time-wasting fun clicking around, using hypertext links, moving seamlessly from a website in East Cheam to one in Hawaii – and you don't even need your Bermuda shorts.

(As an aside, don't you think it odd how we talk of 'going to' a website rather than, say, 'loading it' or 'looking at it' or 'checking it out'? After all, we don't leave our computer screen.)

Anyway, the Web was invented – as with the Internet – for another use entirely. In fact, Tim Berners-Lee, a British scientist working at the European Laboratory for Particle Physics in Geneva, probably couldn't have foreseen the culture shift his invention would bring about, when he decided to develop a system for sharing information among teams of scientists who were geographically far apart. It grew quickly, of course, and eventually supported a large business marketplace.

There's now a www Consortium based at the Massachusetts Institute of Technology, which oversees further developments of the Web.

●

The telephone Some have been known to call it the instrument of the Devil. However, there's at least one good thing to be said about it, according to the American journalist Fran Lebowitz in *Social Studies (1981)*: 'The telephone is a good way to talk to people without having to offer them a drink.'

Whether the instrument of devils or angels, the telephone consists of a diaphragm that the voice (or any noise, come to that) impacts upon

 in the form of sound waves, converting those vibrations into electrical impulses, which scoot along the wires and get converted back into sound by a diaphragm at the other end. Of course, it's capable of more than just that, as we see from the world of mobile phones, which convert signals into, and out of, microwave energy, causing concern in some circles about the possible effects on the brain, particularly in children. The theory is that, because the skull is thinner in children and the brain is still developing, any harmful radiation could have a greater effect than on an adult's brain.

If the old-fashioned, hard-wired telephone was thought of as the instrument of the Devil, then the mobile phone must come in for ten times the antipathy. While it's one of the handiest forms of telephone invented so far – and can now be used in all sorts of ways, including sending text, receiving news and sports results and surfing the World Wide Web – it does come in for criticism from those people who prefer train journeys not to be disturbed by a chorus of chirruping and cheeping as mobile phones begin to sound around them.

•

The telescope A Dutch spectacle maker called Hans Lippershey is reputed to have been the inventor of the telescope. He constructed a simple model in 1608, but the first one on record was exhibited by Galileo (1564–1642), the Italian astronomer, in 1609. The German astronomer Johannes Kepler (1571–1630) took things a bit further when he used two convex lenses and discovered the principle of the astronomical telescope.

It was the English mathematician and physicist Isaac Newton (1642–1727) who constructed the first reflecting telescope in 1668.

Mirrors played a big part in subsequent telescope technology, with the French physician and astronomer Laurent Cassegrain's invention of a telescope, in about 1672, that used a convex mirror instead of a concave one.

Then the English astronomer William Herschel (1738–1822) tilted the mirror in his own telescope and positioned the eyepiece in such a way that it didn't block the incident rays. However, his telescopes were very big: about 4

feet (122 centimetres) in diameter, with a tube about 40 feet (12.2 metres) long.

Telescopes that were capable of accurately photographing large areas of sky didn't come about until 1931, when an Estonian-born German optician called Bernhard Schmidt invented a device that reflected and refracted.

The largest reflecting telescope in the world is the Keck telescope at Mauna Kea Observatory in Hawaii.

But the name that immediately springs to mind when thinking of telescopes is Hubble, which has the advantage of being above the distorting atmosphere of Earth. The Hubble was launched in 1990, but had a misshapen primary mirror, which didn't reflect too well on its designers. It was repaired in 1993, although it had sent back some pretty impressive pictures before the repair job. More orbiting laboratories have been sent up since then.

One of the biggest stories concerning telescopes in recent years came at a meeting of the American Astronomical Society in June 2000, when a team of 30 astronomers presented a 3-D map of the universe that was four times larger than any previous map.

The map is, rather impressively, known as the 2dF (2-Degree Field) Galaxy Redshift Survey, and it was produced by the Anglo-Australian Telescope near Coonabarabran, Australia.

•

The CD-ROM When we first used one of these in our office computer, it sounded like a spin dryer. Now they sound a lot smoother and go a lot faster and, some would say, we'd be lost without them.

You can get not only games on CD-ROM, but lots of reference materials, too. That's where, for writers, researchers and editors, for instance, they really come into their stride. Type a word or phrase into its on-board search engine, and within seconds you are directed to the article, picture, video footage or piece of animation you require. With all those hot links doing the work of cross-referencing, you can skip to another article (or even a built-in dictionary) to look something up and then return to your reading.

While there's a nice sense of romance in taking down a dusty old volume of *Britannica* or *Crockford's* or the *Shorter Oxford* from the high bookshelf, blowing if off, adjusting your half-moon spectacles and peering professorially at the pages, while a coal fire burns with an invitingly convivial and cheerful snugness in the hearth, there's nothing like the clinical efficiency and cold, detached slickness of the CD-ROM drive, with its cheerless hum, spewing words and images onto your computer screen, splattering information before your astounded eyes with latest-generation digital deftness.

As you lower yourself into your armchair and hear the faint creak of the ancient leather, while affectionately caressing the pages of your treasured tome of wisdom, think of the six hundred megabytes of digital storage and the laser optics that allow your computer to read the data on a CD-ROM.

As the genial fire crackles soothingly in the grate, sending its flickering light to play up and down the walls, think of the bright computer screen with its thousands of pixels making up the garishly coloured image.

The 'CD' bit stands for 'compact disc', while 'ROM', as everyone knows, is 'read-only memory', which means you can't change the data when you find there's something you profoundly disagree with.

A CD-ROM is similar to a WORM (yes, another acronym), which means 'write once, read many', so you create the thing yourself. There are also optical read-write devices, so you can make your own CD-ROM of all the riveting stuff you keep on your computer.

Ah, pass the dusty *Britannica* and bring us a cup of cocoa.

•

The automatic pilot This is sometimes called 'autopilot' or 'autohelmsman' and is used not only in aeroplanes, but also on ships and spacecraft. It's a handy device that allows the craft to be piloted without the hands-on intervention of the aircrew.

The simplest type of automatic pilot is the steering vane used by the single-handed yachtsman. It's set to the wind and, provided the wind stays constant, so does the yacht. Deviation while the yachtsman is asleep can, of course, lead to all sorts of interesting encounters.

The more complex autopilots on aircraft use deviations in pitch or roll, detected by a vertical gyroscope, while a directional gyroscope detects changes in heading (or direction, to you and us). Any variations from the selected flight plan are fed in the form of corrective signals to an aeroplane's ailerons, rudder and elevator.

The term 'automatic pilot' – as in 'I'm on automatic pilot' – is also a way of saying you're so exhausted that you're going through your day like an automaton.

•

The lightning rod Lightning will find the path of least resistance. So the lightning rod was invented. It stands higher than the building or structure it's meant to protect, so that any passing lightning will go to the rod first and be discharged into the ground.

The lightning rod was invented by Benjamin Franklin (1706–90), the American printer, scientist and diplomat. He'd been doing electrical experiments for some years before he did the famous one with the kite, in 1752, that led to the lightning rod's invention.

•

The gimbal A word valued because it sounds sort of rather nice and silly, but its real use is to describe a device used in gyroscopes. In fact, without a gimbal, it's doubtful a gyroscope could exist. That's why pilots of aircraft are very pleased indeed that the gimbal exists, because it is upon the gyroscope that the success of the more complex automatic pilots depend.

A gimbal is a device used for keeping instruments such as compasses and chronometers vertical while at sea or in the air. It works by having a pivoted ring at right angles to one or two others. Very handy and also known as a gimmal, but that doesn't sound half as nice as gimbal.

Intellectual and Philosophical Ideas and Other Isms and Ologies

You can really impress people with isms and ologies. Remember those 'Idiot's Guide to …' and 'Bluff Your Way Into …' books that would give you a smattering of the subject in question? Very handy if you wanted to dip your toe into a topic – and, of course, they had the advantage of being funny and irreverent at the same time.

Anyway, to whet your appetite for these mind-bending ways of thinking, we've put together this little compilation of isms and ologies. But, just in case you start to feel inferior because you didn't think of them first, take consolation from the words of the American journalist Fran Lebowitz in *Social Studies (1981)*:

'Original thought is like original sin: both happened before you were born to people you could not have possibly met.'

•

Epistemology You want to know how to know? Epistemology should do the trick. It's that branch of philosophy that looks at the problems surrounding knowledge itself – its limits, what brings it about, how somebody who knows is related to what's known.

Epistemology has been around, we suppose, since the Greek Sophists began to question the reliability of knowledge way back in the fifth century BC.

Our favourite is Georgias (c. 485–c. 380 BC), who said nothing existed; if it did, you couldn't know it; if you could, you couldn't communicate it. Now there's a mind-boggling concept!

Protagorus (c. 480–c. 411 BC) was another interesting philosopher. He said your opinions

were no better than anybody else's, because each person is the best judge of his or her own experience.

Then along comes that most famous of philosophers, Plato (c. 428–c. 347 BC), who proposed his idea of 'forms'. Forms are invisible ideas, so that the thing itself – horse, rock, spoon, fork – is an imperfect version of the pure form of itself that exists in mathematics and philosophy.

So you couldn't know from handling them the intrinsic nature of things – their thingness – but only through meditating on the pure form.

Aristotle (384–322 BC) thought abstract knowledge superior, but thought it originated in sense perception.

Grown men have been reduced to tears thinking about all this stuff. Suffice it to say that, by the seventeenth century, philosophers had begun to see reasoning as the main means of acquiring knowledge.

Monadology This is the name of a book as well as being an ology. According to Gottfried Leibniz (1646–1716), the world – in fact the whole universe – is made up of monads. These are infinitely small units that are 'simple' in that they're not composite.

A monad is a basic, infinitely small unit of force, smaller than which you just can't get. It's also a microcosm of the cosmic whole that it's a part of.

A monad is definitely not to be confused with a nomad, which is an anagram of monad and moves around a lot.

Seriously, though, believe it or not, these monads can actually perceive. But those that perceive the most clearly come to be the souls and minds of human beings. Those with the least clarity of perception end up as inanimate objects, such as rocks.

Leibniz called God the Monad of Monads, so presumably he (or she) must be a composite.

This organic–spiritual view of Leibniz began

another ism: idealism. His view of the world, the universe and everything as an infinite number of monads is contained in his book, called *The Monadology*, although the original title was *The Principles of Philosophy* (which doesn't have you reaching for a dictionary); it was written in 1714 when Leibniz was nearly 70.

•

Idealism   The world cannot be known, except through the mind. That just about sums up Idealism. At its most extreme, it's solipsism – the idea that nothing outside of your own mind exists.

However, most idealists don't go that far, but acknowledge that there is a world out there. They say that you need a mind to make sense of it. The human mind has, too, been responsible for the existence of some things – such as the law, mathematics, the arts, religion.

Plato's idealism involved the existence of

forms (*see* **Epistemology**) – idealized notions of the objects they're represented by. So every stone is an idealized form of a stone, every dog an idealized form of a dog.

The Irish philosopher and clergyman George Berkely (1685–1753) was verging on the solipsistic when he postulated that everything perceived was part of the mind, and any idea of the existence of external objects required to bring about that perception was nothing but speculation. Just whose mind he thought he was a part of, goodness only knows.

The German philosopher Immanuel Kant (1724–1804) refined all this by saying you can't know a thing by what it is, only by the way it appears. In other words, you can know the absolute truth of nothing.

Then came G.W.F. Hegel (1770–1831), another German philosopher, who said that all things were intelligible. Our highest achievements, such as the creation of the state, our culture and our art, were not, as some had said, products of a naturally occurring process in the mind, but of the activity of the free intellect.

•

Solipsism Believe it or not, there are philosophers who still argue the merits of this belief that only one's own mind and its contents can be said to exist or be known.

It's a bit like the brain-in-a-vat theory that has you as a brain in a vat of chemical nutrients, being fed all the data that make you believe this, that and the other are happening to you, or to someone else. The ideas of sky, birds, the ground, the car, the mobile phone, other people, other people's mobile phones, lavatory seats and policemen's helmets are being fed to you. Yet the experience – just like a very vivid dream – is there in your brain. This book you hold in your hands may be a few gigabytes of data stimulating a ganglion of neurones in your hippocampus. Are you sure you have a body?

Well, at least you know you exist – even if you are a brain in a vat. You know this because you are, after all, experiencing reading this book, and you have to have a mind in order to have experiences. Descartes' famous saying *'Cogito, ergo sum'*, meaning 'I think, therefore I am', indicated that one needs to exist in order to have experiences. Well, thank goodness for that, is all we can say. After all, it comes as a relief to know that you exist.

·

Structuralism 'Language is not a form and not a substance,' claimed Ferdinand de Saussure (1857–1913), a Geneva-born Swiss linguist. But it's in his linguistics that structuralism has its roots.

It's a European movement, which began in France in the mid-fifties, in which language plays a big role. Indeed, it is a dissection of language that tries to show how everything is made up of smaller constituent parts. Even a myth, according to this school, is made up of constituents, as the French anthropologist Claude Lévi-Strauss attempted to demonstrate in a paper called 'The Structural Study of Myth', which appeared in the *Journal of American Folklore* in 1955. He maintained that a myth is made up of constituent units, just as the rest of language is, and has to be related to a huge network of meaning. So, everything is seen within a vast system of meanings or 'significations', and these can be defined only within the context of the system of which they are a part.

Still following?

Anyway, mind-bending as it may seem, structuralism is another Great Idea, and, if you can memorize the few and simple words we've used to describe it, you can bluff your way into any intellectual conversation at parties.

•

Postmodernism This is where things get complicated. There's postmodernism in art and architecture, dance, literature, philosophy, the analysis of contemporary society, painting, music, sculpture, the sciences, theology, aesthetics, anthropology – and a few other things you'll no doubt think of.

In fact, as you would imagine, the term is used to refer to a rebellion towards, a rejection of, or a re-examination of what came immediately before it. You guessed it: modernism. We'll look at just a couple of examples, otherwise it starts to get tedious.

The term 'postmodernism' is thought to have first been used in the 1970s in the context of architecture, and referred to a reaction to the highly austere functionalism of the modernist movement.

In art and architecture, postmodernism is a phenomenon of the late twentieth century, and combines some elements of the modern (materials, techniques and forms) with motifs and ideas from earlier periods. Of course, modernism was itself a reaction to traditional forms and came in the early part of the twentieth century. So we see some traditional elements put back into things in the form of postmodernism.

Postmodernism in dance was, again, a reaction to modernism, which was a reaction to traditional forms. In fact, in many cases, the only thing modernists had in common was that they were rebelling against tradition and wanting to explore new forms and re-examine the fundamental principles behind their chosen medium. So, when you look at it like that, whether modernism could be called a movement is anybody's guess.

Postmodernism in literature is notoriously difficult to define. The term denotes a whole host of styles – again, a response to modernism, but partly as a result of post-industrial mass-production. And what makes it harder to pin down is that the term often denotes a reluctance to give a label to certain types of writing or art.

Gravity

Gravity is the force of attraction that moves or tends to move objects towards the centre of a celestial body, such as the earth or moon. Modern understanding of gravity is principally indebted to Sir Isaac Newton (1642-1727), who at the age of twenty-three moved from Cambridge to the countryside in order to escape the plague. Watching an apple fall from a tree led him to question how far the downward force acting upon the apple actually reached, and from that he recognized that the force causing the apple to fall also kept the moon in orbit around the earth. (The force of attraction that objects exert upon one another because of their mass [weight, the amount of matter of which they are composed] is called **gravitation**.) From this he formulated his Theory of Gravitation, which states that the gravitational force between two objects is directly proportional to their mass, and is dependent upon their distance from each

other. Since, however, his
original theory was based
upon an inaccurate cal-
culation of the earth's
radius, Newton did
nothing with it, even
though he later learned
the true measurement of
the earth's radius. It was

left to the English astronomer Edmund Halley
(1656-1742) to persuade Newton to publish his
findings on gravity and motion (among other
matters), which he did in 1687 in a book
generally known as *Principia Mathematica*, a
work still considered to be one of the greatest
single contributions to the study of science.
Newton's Theory remained the dominant
work on the laws of gravity until 1915, when
the German (later American) physicist Albert
Einstein (1879-1955) published his theory of
gravitation, known as the General Theory of
Relativity (*see* **E=mc²**).

E=mc² Contrary to popular belief, this well-known formula does not define or describe relativity 9q.v.). Einstein's neat little equation is in fact only a corrollary of his Special Theory of Relativity of 1905, which itself  forms a special case in his General Theory of Relativity (1916). He himself did not consider the formula to be especialy worthy of attention, seeing it as part of a much greater whole.

•

The thesaurus When you want to be regarded as really intellectual, academic, well educated, well-read, erudite, learned, bookish, donnish, intelligent, highbrow, scholarly and studious you could do worse than study, investigate, research, examine, analyse, review, survey, scrutinize and enquire into a thesaurus.

What a handy, useful, helpful, practical,

functional, expedient, easy-to-use, neat, convenient idea it is, when you want that extra word, term, expression or remark.

It was one Peter Mark Roget (1779–1869) who compiled, gathered, collected, accumulated, amassed, assembled, put together, collated, marshalled, organized and systematized lists of words, so that a useful synonym could easily be found by those writers and speakers who actually cared about their use of language.

His book's full title is *Thesaurus of English Words and Phrases*, and it was put together in 1852 after his retirement as a doctor, although he'd been compiling and classifying words as early as 1805. It works on a different principle from the dictionary-style thesaurus that's more prevalent today. You had to look up the word for which you wanted a synonym in a long index, and it would point you in the right direction. The words in the body of the thesaurus were not alphabetical, but arranged in classifications. This produced a soporific effect as you found yourself performing a rambling read, moving smoothly from one classification to another until you were miles away from the synonyms you were looking for.

There are, of course, those people who don't need to go to the index, but can go straight to the classification and find the desired synonym. Which probably makes it more fun to use and browse through than the dictionary-style thesaurus.

●

The dictionary To judge by tabloid and regional newspapers and utterances on most radio stations and networks, you could be forgiven for thinking no one uses this handy device any more. Yet they seem to sell enormously well, and you can usually see huge piles of them in high street bookshops and can swear that new editions seem to come out far more frequently than they ever used to do. Such is the nature of language in the age of instant communication that words and their usage are constantly on the move.

So the dictionary comes high on our list of Great Ideas.

We all know what a dictionary is, of course, but there are also specialist dictionaries dealing with particular subjects. The chap we associate with modern dictionaries is Dr Samuel Johnson (1709–84), the English critic, essayist and poet who gave us such immortal, quotable and often pithy aphorisms as 'There are few minds to which tyranny is not delightful' and 'The whole of life is but keeping away the thoughts of death. We'll come back to Johnson later.

But there's evidence of dictionaries among the Assyrians in the seventh century BC, which were found in the library of the king, Ashurbanipal at Nineveh, inscribed on clay tablets – in columns, too.

Several specialist and general dictionaries are to be found in various cultures throughout history. The first attempt to put all of the Arabic vocabulary in one book was made by Khalil ibn Ahmad of Oman, and there's academic dispute over when Hebrew dictionaries came into being, with some scholars saying as early as the eighth century CE and others going for a little later – around the tenth century.

Oddly enough, the Greeks and Romans didn't put together a dictionary of their respective vocabularies, preferring, it seems, to compile a number of specialist dictionaries, instead: glossaries of unusual words or phrases. Appolonius, for instance, during the third century BC put together a dictionary of the words and terms used by Homer of *Iliad* fame.

The Italian monk Ambrogio Calepino put together one of the first bilingual dictionaries in 1502. It was originally Latin–Greek, but was later extended and included French, Spanish and Italian.

We have to wait until 1612 to see dictionaries in the vernacular (as distinct from Latin), with such works as *Vocabulario degli Accademici della Crusca* in 1612 and the *Dictionnaire* of the French Academy in 1694. Many more scholarly works followed.

But the first dictionary compiled in the English language was thought to be the *Promptorium Parvulorum Sive Clericorum*, which means *Storehouse for Children or Clerics*, which was printed in 1449, having been compiled in 1440. It was put together by a monk known as Geoffrey the Grammarian in Norfolk, England. It contained about ten thousand words with Latin equivalents.

The first lexicographer to produce a dictionary that gave English definitions of English words was Robert Cawdry, in *A Table Alphabeticall … of Hard Usuall Wordes* in 1604. But we're still in the realm of unusual and difficult words. The dictionaries we're familiar with today contain most common words, from the single-letter variety, such as the indefinite article 'a', to the wonderful 'floccinaucinihilipilification' (yep, it exists – look it up).

The first to define common words was John Kersey's *New English Dictionary*, in 1702.

Samuel Johnson comes onto the scene in 1755 with *A Dictionary of the English Language*, in two volumes. As well as standardizing spelling and punctuation, it also leaned heavily on quotations to help understanding.

The handiest dictionaries for writers these days, of course, are to be found on a CD-ROM or in a format copyable to your hard drive (assuming you're using a computer to write). Much quicker than leafing through all those gossamer-thin pages.

•

The gods Most of us are familiar with that aphorism of Voltaire (1694–1778): 'If God did not exist, it would be necessary to invent him.' Certainly, when we look at the many types of god that have existed, one wonders how they

came about and, indeed, were actually believed in as thinking, performing entities who could know what was in a mortal's mind.

While science can't explain everything, we do tend to look to it to provide answers, whereas noises in the sky, torrential downpourings, movements of the earth and droughts were around long before science came on the scene, and demanded explanation.

So what could that noise in the sky be but Thor's chariot thundering through the heavens? What could be the explanation behind the failure of the harvest but that old trickster Loki, getting up to his mischief? And what could that giant golden orb up there be but Ra?

One interesting set of deities are the Japanese Seven Gods of Good Fortune (Shichi-fuku-jin), which are thought to bring wealth, health and good fortune. These are quite a modern set compared with some: the cult came into prominence as late as the fifteenth century; and the origins of the seven are mixed, some having been deities, some mere sages; some have Chinese roots and some Indian. The Seven Gods of Good Fortune are often to be found as the subjects of netsuke figurines, and in other forms of art. One favourite is a picture of the seven in a treasure ship, and it's believed that if you place such a picture under your pillow on the night of 1 January, the first dream of the new year will be a lucky one.

Gods – made by man usually in his own image – have been around since humankind first asked a question. Over the millennia, they have been perceived to exist actually in natural phenomena such as rain and other characteristics of the weather, and in celestial objects, animals and even vegetation.

Opposed to polytheism, which is a belief in many gods and not just those that are parrots, is monotheism, the belief in one god, as favoured by the major religions, such as Judaism, Islam and Christianity – who, share the same god.

While polytheism seems related to a belief in all kinds of supernatural beings – demons, spirits, fairies at the bottom of the garden, vampires and werewolves – it elevates its entities to deities in a personified form, usually belonging to some sort of hierarchy. The most famous polytheistic societies are those of the Ancient Greeks and the Romans, whose gods were parallels. A few examples:

The Greek Aphrodite is the Roman Venus, goddess of beauty and sexual desire. The Greek Cronus is the Roman Saturn, who, as Cronus ruled the Titans as well as the sky, and in Roman mythology was the ruler of agriculture. The god of love is Eros to the Greeks, Cupid to the Romans, while the god of wine and generally having a good time, Dionysus to the Greeks, was Bacchus to the Romans.

The god of the gods, of course, was Zeus to the Greeks, Jupiter to the Romans. Zeus is the youngest son of the Titans, Rhea and Cronus. Cronus had a habit of swallowing whole his children as soon as they were born, because he feared one of them might dethrone him. So, when Zeus was born, Rhea gave Cronus a rock wrapped in swaddling clothes to swallow and she hid Zeus away.

Gods often had specific purposes and ruled

particular aspects of life on Earth: childbirth, fire, marriage, fertility, sleep, the home, earthquakes, grain, love, the sea, medicine, war, the sky.

•

Marxism   Born in 1818, Karl Marx was perhaps best known for his co-authorship, with Friedrich Engels, of the *Communist Manifesto*, which was published in 1848.

Marx was a German political thinker, one of the most influential people in modern history. That makes him not just a thinker, but a Thinker.

Marx wrote an article for *Rheinische Zeitung*, and then became that paper's editor, criticizing social conditions and getting himself into annoying little spots of bother with the authorities. He had to resign his position in 1843.

He went to Paris and studied lots of clever stuff, such as philosophy and political science and plenty of isms, and it was then that he actually adopted communist beliefs. It was here that he

met Engels, and they decided to collaborate on their analysis of political principles.

Marx was ordered to leave Paris in 1845 because the authorities were becoming a bit jittery about his views and activities, and he settled in Brussels, where he organized a network of revolutionary committees.

Eventually, Karl and Friedrich were commissioned to write a statement of principles in connection with these committees, and thus the *Communist Manifesto* was published in London in 1848. Not long after this *Manifesto* appeared, there were riots in Germany and France, and the Belgian government became anxious about having Marx in the country, so off he was packed, and made his way to Paris and then to the Rhineland. He wasn't too popular here, either: in 1849 he was arrested in Cologne and charged with incitement to armed insurrection. Once more, he was told to pack his bags, and off he went to London, where he devoted his life to trying to build an international communist movement.

Over the years, he wrote *Das Kapital* (in three volumes) and *The Civil War in France* and lots of articles. After his death on 14 March 1883, notes were found indicating that he intended to write a fourth volume of *Das Kapital*.

His grave is in the eastern section of Highgate Cemetery in north London, and, of course, his influence outlived him, and grew along with the Labour movement. His theories – which were to be revived by Lenin and become central to Bolshevism – came, as you'd expect, to be known as Marxism.

So he'd added one more to all the isms he'd studied as a younger man.

Art for Art's Sake

We present, in no particular order, some more isms and similar schools, this time in the world of the arts. It's not an exhaustive guide, but we hope it's entertaining.

•

Impressionism If you want someone to create a perfect image of something, you hire a photographer. If you want to see more of what the artist was seeing, through the filter of his mind, you turn to the Impressionists.

You might say the Impressionists saw the light. This was the basis of their work: the interplay of light and colour, rather than purely representational, formal and academic creations of the old school, such as those approved by the rather dry-sounding *Académie des Beaux-Arts* based in Paris.

This organization sponsored the official salon exhibitions and tended to set the standards for French art.

Impressionism developed in the late nineteenth century in France, but had some of its precursors in England in the form of our beloved Constable and Turner, both landscape painters.

When one or two of the French notables of the time, Claude Monet (1840–1926) and Camille Pissarro (1830–1903), saw the work of Constable and Turner, they were enchanted by the diffusing, vibrant effect of light.

The Impressionists' effect was to be felt far and wide, for, as with any movement, it has its progenitors and its progeny. One notable on whom Impressionism made an impression was James Whistler (1834–1903). Indeed, in that very painting (known popularly as *Whistler's Mother*, but actually called *Arrangement in Black and Grey No. 1: The Artist's Mother*), the rather flat, two-dimensional impression is reminiscent of one of the great exponents of Impressionism, Monet.

Whistler explored tonalities in a series of paintings, concentrating on the interplay of colour, which came to be more important than the subjects themselves.

Others who have been influenced by Impressionism include Walter Sickert, Mary Cassatt, Childe Hassam, Winslow Homer, John Singer Sargent and Giovanni Segantini.

Impressionism also gave rise to an interesting technique called pointillism.

Pointillistic paintings are best viewed from a distance. Instead of using pre-mixed colour, Pointillists dab dots or small strokes of paint on the canvas, juxtaposed with dots or dabs of other colours, so that, when seen from a distance, the work gives off a more vibrant effect, because the final colour seen has been 'mixed' by the eye and the brain.

The heightened luminosity is really based on the colour theories of Impressionism. Georges Seurat (1859–91), known as the founder of Neo-Impressionism exemplified the style.

Alice Perhaps we'll never know what Charles Lutwidge Dodgson (1832–98) was inspired by, when he wrote about Mad Hatters, talking eggs, White Rabbits and Cheshire Cats. As Lewis Carroll, what he did create was the first children's story written from a child's point of view. Alice, then, if for no reason other than this, was another Great Idea.

So enchanted was the family friend to whom Carroll read his story (written for Alice Liddell, the young daughter of the classicist Henry George Liddell) of Alice and her Wonderland adventures that he was asked to write it down, which, of course, he did. He went back to the text, expanding here, giving it a snip and a tuck there. The result: one of the most widely read pieces of children's literature to be found then or since. Carroll's writing departed from all the stuffy moralistic nonsense of the time and brought us real nonsense: the world of fantasy, of impossibly engaging and charming – and some not so charming – characters and surreal situations.

Alice's Adventures in Wonderland (1865) is still a favourite – and not just among children, for it's often been studied by academics. There was a sequel, equally well known: *Through the Looking Glass (1871)*.

The English cartoonist and illustrator Sir John Tenniel (1820–1914) provided 42 illustrations for *Wonderland* and 50 for *Looking Glass*, and such was Carroll's confidence in Tenniel's wonderfully creative work that, in some cases, he left it to the artist to decide what animal to depict, and Carroll adjusted the text accordingly.

•

Cubism Everything called an ism seems to be a reaction to a previous ism. Cubism is no exception.

While Impressionism was a reaction against the more formalized painting styles that preceded it, so was Cubism – but that was also a revolt against Impressionism, too, with its emphasis on colour and light and its lack of form.

Cubism – a twentieth-century art movement – attempted to break things down into geometric shapes, often interlocking, and occasionally showing aspects of the subject from different angles, which wouldn't be possible it the subject were viewed in real life.

Cubism is the precursor to abstract and non-objective art, and had a wide influence, two of its proponents being Pablo Picasso (1881–1973) and Georges Braque (1882–1963).

•

The diatonic scale By the late nineteenth century, this handy little musical device was disappearing from Western music at a great rate of crotchets. But the beauty of the diatonic scale is that it has only seven notes in it – yet it's called an octave!

Imagine that all the notes on a piano are white ones, and you don't have to think about those intrusive black ones that give you an interval of a semitone (assuming you haven't jumped from another black one, that is). Wouldn't pianos be so much easier to play? Any one can pick out a tune on all the white notes –if you're in the key of C (in any other key you'll be forced to do battle with some of those black notes, too).

But then along came the chromatic scale to spoil it all. That's the one based on twelve notes instead of seven, and we were forced to think of the notes between the notes. Why does life have to be so complicated?

Some composers have even experimented

with 'microtonal' scales – scales with intervals smaller than a semitone. (To get between a black note and a white note you need fingers the size of ants' legs.) And, when you consider that there are pentatonic scales (of five notes, and found mainly in folk and non-Western music) and heptatonic scales (six notes), you just hanker for that nice simple diatonic: doh, ray, me, fah, so, lah, te, do.

•

The piano Everyone in the Western world has, at some time, either played or sung to one of these versatile instruments, whether in a bar or at parties at home. Elsewhere on the cultural scale, pianos are to be found creating the most exquisite sounds from the concert platform, or issuing forth refreshing and innovative music in jazz and rock combos.

They are capable of drama and infinite subtlety, and often allow their practitioners to display astonishing feats of dexterity.

There are grand pianos and pianos that aren't so grand. There used to be one of the latter – an upright – in just about every living room in the country. Piano lessons were, it seems, taken as a matter of course.

The instrument as we know it was born of the harpsichord and the clavichord, as far as its keyboard is concerned. It was also derived from the dulcimer in that it had hammers and strings.

Its hammer-and-lever action, though, allows it to be played softly (piano) or loudly (forte). That's how it got its full name: the pianoforte.

The earliest model our exhaustive investigations have been able to pin down was in 1709 and was called the *gravicembalo col pian e forte*, which in Italian means 'harpsichord with soft and loud'. The man credited with inventing the joanna was Bartolomeo Cristofori, a Florentine harpsichord maker.

Pianos more resembling those of today began to emerge around 1760, when a group of German piano makers went to London and, with John Broadwood and other piano makers, established the English school. Broadwood (1732–1812) founded the company of the same name, which was the leading firm of piano makers in the late seventeenth and early eighteenth centuries.

There was also a French school, founded by Sébastien Érard (1752–1831) in the 1790s.

Over the years that followed, numerous improvements were made to the piano,

including pedals, which produce changes in the sound quality. The loud pedal lifts all the dampers from the keys, so the sound is sustained. The soft pedal either shifts the hammers closer to the strings to make the impact less, or shifts them slightly to one side, so that less contact is made with the strings.

There's sometimes a third pedal in between those two. That great comic musician Victor Borge once said the pedal in the middle was there to separate the two at either side.

John Cage (1912–92), an American avant-garde composer, invented something called the 'prepared piano', in which pencil erasers, screws and other foreign objects are put between the strings. This does just what pianists are taught to try to hide: it emphasizes the percussive action of the piano.

The most famous names we associate with the joanna are Mozart, Beethoven, Chopin, Liszt, Clara Schumann, her husband, Robert, Anton Rubinstein, Ignace Paderewski, Josef Hofmann,

Arthur Rubinstein, Sergei Rachmaninov, Artur Schnabel, Dame Myra Hess, Walter Gieseking, Guiomar Novaes, Emil Gilels, Sviatoslav Richter, Claudio Arrau, Rudolf Serkin, Vladimir Horowitz, Alicia de Larrocha, Alfred Brendel, Glenn Gould, Van Cliburn, Murray Perahia and Vladimir Ashkenazy.

Oh, and Russ Conway.

•

The limerick

The word 'limerick' comes from a refrain in a popular song of the 1890s, when it was first applied to the verse of the English humorist and painter, Edward Lear (1812–88). It follows the strict rhyme scheme of A, A, B, B, A, and a specific scansion, in that in lines 1, 2 and 5 it has three metrical feet: the first iambic, leading to two anapaestic. 'Feet' are the metrical units in a line: count the stresses – that usually tells you how many metrical feet there are in a line of verse. An iamb is a metric foot: it gives you two syllables, the first unstressed and the second stressed (de-DA). An anapaest is a three-syllable foot that goes de-de-DA.

So now you know.

Limericks have almost always been used (and indeed Lear himself wrote a lot of them) to express humour – much of it lavatory humour for most of the twentieth century, and, it has to be said, they do lend themselves to the seedier sentiments that can be expressed in rhyme.

And that rhythm and rhyme scheme couldn't really lend itself to anything else. It has a jauntiness that invites humorous writing – and we've all heard jokes told in limerick form.

•

Iambic pentameter One wonders what William Shakespeare would have done without iambic pentameter.

For what an iamb is, *see* **The limerick**. As for pentameter, that just means there are five metrical feet to the line: de-DA, de-DA, de-DA, de-DA, de-DA: 'The moving finger writes, and having writ …' Iambic pentameter is one of the – if not the – most widely used verse forms, and entire, seemingly never-ending, tales have been told using it. Most of Shakespeare's stuff is written in blank verse, which is non-rhyming iambic pentameter. For instance:

> *The nightingale, if she should sing by day …*
> *What angel wakes me from my flowery bed?*
> *The lunatic, the lover and the poet …*

Iambic pentameter was used by poets writing in English from the sixteenth to the twentieth centuries, and is still to be seen in more modern works.

The beauty of this form for reading aloud is that it allows for variation. No two readers will interpret a line alike. You don't have to say, 'The LUnaTIC, the LOVer AND the POet', but the impression of the verse form will be detectable, even if subtly modified by your own interpretation of the line.

Well, it won't win any prizes, but illustrates the point (in an ABAB rhyme scheme, too).

Oh, the quotation in the first paragraph of this entry is from *All's Well That Ends Well*. But you knew that already.

•

The malapropism The malapropism was invented by Richard Brinsley Sheridan (1751–1816) and used with great wit in his play *The Rivals*. It's the misapplication of a word (by a character called Mrs Malaprop), usually to humorous effect – and comics and writers of comedy, it seems, can't get by without the occasional example.

Mrs Malaprop's Latin-based name means 'inappropriate' or 'badly to the purpose' (*mal à propos*). Some of her own are:

- 'Oh, my dear Sir Anthony!
  You are a misanthropy!'
- 'She's as headstrong as an allegory on the banks of the Nile.'
- 'He is the very pineapple of politeness.'

While malapropisms are used in comic material, they're often unintentional, as Philip Norman reported in *The Times* in May 1985: he wrote of a miners' leader who called his bosses 'totally incontinent', and a parishioner who, having failed to hear what was being said in church, complained to the vicar that the building had poor 'agnostics'.

In more recent times, President George W. Bush is supposed to have spoken of keeping 'good relations with the Grecians' (Greeks).

There are many literary devices, of course, some for comedy and some to evoke other emotions, but dear Mrs Malaprop has given us one of the best.

•

Last words Last words are a super idea, because they mean you can have your friends put it about that some witty remark it took you years to think of was uttered with total spontaneity and clarity of mind as you grunted your last grunt and gasped your last gasp. Still, some of them can be quite entertaining.

King George V's last words were alleged to be 'Bugger Bognor', when some bright spark remarked at the King's deathbed, 'Cheer up, your majesty, you will soon be at Bognor again.'

Socrates' last words were a hoot – although we don't know whether he said them before he'd swallowed the hemlock in CE 399, or afterwards, and paralysis and whatever else had set in.

'Crito,' he said, 'we owe a cock to

Aesculapius; please pay it and don't forget it.'

Lord Palmerston (1784–1865) got it about right when he said, 'Die, my dear Doctor – that's the last thing I shall do!'

Vespasian, or, to give him his full name, Titus Flavius Sabinus Vespasianus, who died in CE 79, said, 'An emperor ought to die standing.'

'Greetings! We win!' gasped Pheidippides (or Philippides, take your pick), who died in 490 BCE after running back to Athens from Marathon with news of the victory over the Persians.

One of the best – and it's one of the best known, too – comes from Captain Lawrence Oates (1880–1912), who, on Scott's last expedition, said, 'I am just going outside and may be some time.'

Dying's not all it's cracked up to be – at least that's what the British biographer and literary critic Lytton Strachey (1880–1932) thought. He said, on his deathbed, 'If this is dying, then I don't think much of it.'

The famous last words of the brilliant wit and playwright Oscar Wilde (1854–1900) were said of his wallpaper, which he didn't seem to like very much: 'One of us must go.'

A Union general called John Sedgwick said, just before he was killed by enemy fire at the battle of Spotsylvania in the American Civil War in 1864, 'They couldn't hit an elephant at this distance.'

Nice one to end this entry on. It's from the American psychologist and drug pioneer Timothy Leary (1920–96), who was famously fired when he started fooling about with consciousness-altering substances: 'Why not? Why not? Why not? Yeah.'

Transport and Associated Ideas

Every human action concerns moving something from one place to another. Think about it. So we'd be lost without a means of moving things – and ourselves – from A to B, whether it's the invention of the wheel or the rockets of the space age.

•

The bicycle It wasn't always thus called. There were a number of precursors to what we now know as the bicycle, or bike, and one was the velocipede-fast feet. They became popular in France in 1855, and the modern name for this brilliant, environment-friendly, healthy-to-use contraption came about in 1869 or thereabouts.

However, as early as the second half of the

seventeenth century, crude, wooden-beamed vehicles with wheels attached had been popular. There was no handlebar, and you sat astride this thing on a cushion (an absolute must on cobbled streets) and pushed the contrivance along with your feet. As you can see, you got no multiplication of speed as you do with geared vehicles, but it was a start – and great for going downhill.

The first steerable bike was invented by a German nobleman in 1816, and was called the 'draisine', after the name of its inventor. Improvements followed in Britain, Germany and France.

Pedals and driving levers were attached to these vehicles, and other similar improvements were made until 1846, when a Scotsman devised a better machine, called the 'dalzell', that was widely used in England.

Then came the velocipede, which is seen as the direct precursor to the modern bike. Wheels and frame were made of wood, but the tyres were of iron. Add that to the cobbled streets, and you'd certainly want a cushioned seat! No wonder that, in England, this thing was known as the boneshaker.

Smarting buttocks had to wait until 1869 before solid rubber tyres mounted on metal rims came into being, but they must have been aching for someone to invent the pneumatic tyre. And it was at this time that, as we've seen, the term bicycle was used.

In 1873, James Starley of Coventry produced the 'ordinary', or the high-wheeled bicycle, with the front wheel three times as wide as the rear. These were also known as penny-farthings.

Spring seats, ball bearings, weldless steel tubing and the pneumatic tyre were the improvements that were added over the following years, bringing the bike further towards the shape that's familiar to us today – including having wheels of the same size and the rider closer to the ground.

Today's bikes are different again, with many developments added for sporting purposes and to make machines lighter, more manoeuvrable, safer and more comfortable, with multiple gears to enable riders to get up hills more easily and really crank up the mph when they're on the flat or going downhill.

The bicycle needs no fuel, except a hearty breakfast for the rider, and less maintenance than a motor car. And, of course, it doesn't belch out fumes.

There are other self-propelled modes of transport, of course, such as the skateboard and the micro-scooter, but they were also crazes, so you'll find them in that section of the book.

•

Steam Not a Great Idea per se, we admit, but a wonderful example of something that has produced power and romance, as well as noise.

A few facts about steam:

- steam is water in the vapour state, and it is produced at roughly 100°C at sea level
- if water is boiled under pressure the boiling point rises
- pure steam is actually an invisible gas and what you see when the kettle boils is tiny droplets of water taken up with the steam

Two Great Ideas came from this gas: the steamboat and the steam engine.

They must have had a lot of fun in those days of the steam-powered vessel – steamboat races, entertainment on board. The first steam-powered vessel was in 1786, when a small steamboat was launched on the Delaware river by an inventor called John Fitch (1743–98). Along came Robert Fulton (1765–1815), another inventor, with the first successful paddle steamer in 1807. Soon, boats like this could be seen in the UK and USA in both inland and coastal waters.

A common sight on American waters in the 1800s and early 1900s was a race between two

paddle steamers. Some steamboats – showboats – put on theatre entertainment up and down the Mississippi.

The first piston engine, in France in 1690, was used for pumping water (probably to get it into the boiler so it could produce the steam to drive the engine that pumped the water that …). But what really gets the sentiment up to steam is the locomotive.

The first of these came in 1804, made in England by the Cornwall-born inventor Richard Trevithic (1771–1833). Several more locos were built during subsequent years, mainly used in mining, and the first to carry both freight and passengers made its maiden journey in 1829, the year that George Stephenson (1781–1848), the English railway engineer, built his famous Rocket. It was simply ages before one of these things put a man on the moon, but we have to give him ten out of ten for effort. This Rocket was land-based – well, rail-based – and it won a competition sponsored by the Liverpool and

Manchester Railway. It could pull three times its own weight.

Loco trials were taking place in America at this time, and all kinds of improvements were made until we got something looking like the steam engines that we find so romantic today.

Steam provided the driving power for locos up to around 1940, when other forms began to be used, such as diesel and electric.

And a romantic era steamed off into a nostalgic sunset.

•

The motor car They were originally called 'horseless carriages', in keeping with the verbal inventiveness of the late Victorians. You'd think they'd have come up with something a bit snazzier. Anyway, they looked like nothing on Earth – although, to the folks around at that time, they looked very much like carriages without horses, but with an extra bit, called an

engine, to take the old nag's place.

The horseless carriage was America's first internal-combustion car, and was developed by a pair of brothers called Charles and Frank Duryea in 1893. Later that same year, Henry Ford ('you can have any colour as long as it's black') came along with his experimental car – and the world hasn't looked back since.

Now we have the school run, pollution, noise, road rage, traffic jams, road accidents, whiplash injuries, speed cameras, traffic cops, parking wardens, road tax, escalating fuel prices, dodgy second-hand-car dealers …

Not that the car's that modern. Leonardo da Vinci (1452–1519) looked at ideas for a self-propelled vehicle, and in the seventeenth century there were wind-powered carriages using sails or kites. If you want to be really pernickety about the genesis of the motor car, maybe you ought to go back to 1769, when Nicolas-Joseph Cugnot (1725–1804), a French pioneer of steam traction, used his expertise to make a steam-powered vehicle. This idea caught on to an extent, and was developed over the next hundred years, particularly in the UK, but it never really achieved what you might call mass popularity. Anyway, it wasn't going to be that long before the internal-combustion engine made possible the precursor to the motor car as we know it today. That began – broadly speaking – when the engine became front-mounted and the vehicle began to look like a machine in its own right, rather than something that had been cobbled together. A combination of advancing technology, consumer demand and economic conditions has seen the meteoric rise of car ownership, and the enormous variety of shapes and sizes.

What we came to know as 'classic' cars appeared in the 1920s and 1930s, with their sleekness and, in many cases, individual design. More fuel-efficient cars began to be seen in the 1970s and 1980s, largely due to oil shortages, and this trend has continued to the present day, as more people become concerned about the environment and what we're pumping into it.

However, for real fuel efficiency, we recommend the skateboard or the micro-scooter.

The pneumatic tyre This was invented by John Boyd Dunlop, and was extremely good news for buttocks. For, in the days of the solid tyre, the riders of bicycles had to stop every mile or so to get off and rub their sore backsides.

'Tyre' used to refer merely to the protective strip, which was made of metal, around a wheel, but we take it nowadays to refer only to the pneumatic variety.

John Dunlop (1840–1921) invented the first practical pneumatic tyre in 1888, although a chap called R.W. Thompson had produced an earlier version, and patented it in 1845. It was demonstrated and sold, but Dunlop's version obviously won the day. Now the word 'Dunlop' is synonymous with rubber tyres, and the firm of Dunlop is one of the biggest tyre manufactures in the world.

Dunlop began experimenting with hollow rubber tubes filled with air in 1887, in order to make a tricycle ride more comfortable.

An entrepreneur called W. H. Du Cros teamed up with Dunlop to form a company to exploit this amazing new invention, which, of course, had come just at the right time for the emerging motor car.

Don't some people just have all the luck?

The rocket Not Stephenson's (*see* **Steam**), but the stuff of science fiction and fact.

Rockets have been with us – well, with the Chinese, anyway – since the early thirteenth century and were used for military purposes: setting fire to tents and fortifications that arrows couldn't do much damage to. It wasn't long before they were being used for similar purposes in North Africa and Europe.

By the fifteenth century, they had found their way to sea, and were doing serious damage to ships' rigging. By the sixteenth century, they were being used as fireworks. They have, of course, during all phases of their technological evolution, been used to kill people.

But the rocket we immediately think of when we use the word is the space rocket.

Until the days of manned space flight, the payload on the tip of a rocket was usually a weapon or scientific equipment. Then it became the spacecraft. But since the 1950s, when Earth-orbiting stuff was whooshed into space, there have been more than 3,000 launches.

An early landmark in space exploration was the launch of the satellite *Sputnik 1* by the USSR, as it was then, in October 1957. America launched *Explorer 1* three months later.

But it's manned flight that fascinates us. And Yuri Gagarin (1934–68), who became the first man in space. (The Russians called their spacemen cosmonauts, the Americans, astronauts.)

The first space tourist was Dennis Tito, an American millionaire many times over, who was rebuffed by his countrymen at NASA when he wanted to take a vacation on the International Space Station, but was welcomed by the Russians.

He blasted off in late April 2001, and reached the space station on the 30th, returning to Earth on 6 May. It cost him about $20 million, but he said it was worth it.

•

The boat In March 2001, a British chap called Jim Shekhdar became the first person to row unaided across the Pacific. He set off from the coast of Peru on 29 June 2000 and arrived at North Stradbroke Island off the coast of Queensland 274 days later.

Boats have played an essential part in humankind's fascination with and taming of the sea, and the earliest ones were of the raft and dugout variety. The dugout was a rather primitive canoe that was a log hollowed out with basic tools or fire.

The kayak is an early form of canoe, developed by the Inuit and covered in animal skins. The coracle is a rounded version, much in evidence in Wales, where there's a museum devoted to it.

There is evidence that the ancient Egyptians constructed boats with logs or planks.

The more familiar lapstrake (or clinch-built or clinker-built) construction had been well developed by the ninth century CE, mainly in northern Europe and, especially, Scandinavia. This is the method that uses overlapping planks.

There's this thing called smooth-lap construction, whereby the planks are shaped so that they lap, but remain smooth at the seams.

Carvel or smooth-planked construction became popular in the twentieth century, although it's been around a long time and was evident in the Mediterranean in early times, probably a development of the plank boats of the early Egyptians. The reason this method became popular is that it imparts structural strength, useful for boats with motors and fast craft used for racing.

All sorts of materials have been used for making boats, as well as the obvious wood. Aluminium, for instance, was used in Europe as early as 1891, and in America the explorer Walter Wellman used an aluminium boat for his polar expedition in 1894.

There are even boats made of ferroconcrete – closely meshed wire with a spread of cement to make it watertight.

Then there's plastic, of which most boats are built today, including the glass-reinforced variety.

Dangerous Notions

You may think many of these things are not Great Ideas after all, because they're … well, dangerous. But, as with so many things, it's the way they're used that's the moral issue.

(We might draw the line at the atomic bomb, but one day it may be used to propel an oncoming asteroid into another orbit, so we've included it.)

•

The bullet These were originally lead balls a bit smaller in diameter than the barrel of the gun, and they had an annoying tendency to bounce around as they made their way at high speed towards the barrel's end. Consequently, accuracy was somewhat compromised, to say the least.

Rifling was the answer – internal grooves that

imparted spin to the projectile and improved accuracy. But the bullet had to fit the barrel more snugly, and this made for slower loading.

In 1849 Claude-Ettienne Minié, a French army captain, designed a softer bullet that expanded after the explosion in the propellant, making it fit the rifling grooves. Bullets were given a cone shape, and this improved accuracy even further.

It wasn't until the middle of the sixteenth century that people realized that a bullet couldn't possibly describe a straight line – although it was pointed out by an Italian mathematician called Niccolò Tartaglia that greater velocity meant a flatter path.

Modern ballistics techniques are able to tell – by studying minor imperfections on the inside of the barrel of a gun and markings on the bullet – whether a certain bullet was fired by a certain gun. As you can imagine, it's been a great help in forensic science.

Gunpowder A thirteenth-century English monk, Roger Bacon, wrote about this fun substance, so it's been around longer than many people think. In fact, the Chinese were using it several hundred years before that, but it didn't arrive in Europe – probably from the Middle East – until about the early fourteenth century, when a German monk called Bertold Schwarz became the first known person to use it for a projectile.

Bacon, though, was aware of the formula for gunpowder: about 75 per cent potassium nitrate, 15 per cent charcoal and 10 per cent sulphur.

As we know, the Chinese used it for firecrackers – although it's been used since then to far worse ends.

It was manufactured in England by 1334, and in Germany factories were known to exist for its manufacture in 1340. In England, at the time of Elizabeth I, gunpowder could be made only by employees of the crown and strict regulations were in existence from around 1623.

And it's still to be found today to help Guy Fawkes, Fourth of July and New Year celebrations to go with a bang.

The atomic bomb Fission is the name of the process used by the atomic bomb. It is the splitting of nuclei within certain uranium or plutonium isotopes. This is not to be confused with fusion, which are called hydrogen bombs or thermonuclear bombs. These bombs were developed in the 1950s and have not so far been used in warfare.

Fission bombs – also called atom bombs – were what the USA dropped on two Japanese cities, Hiroshima and Nagasaki, in 1945.

Thermonuclear devices do rely on fission, but that is to create enough heat to cause hydrogen isotopes to fuse. They can create far more energy than fission devices and make up most of what's in the world's nuclear stockpiles today.

The physicist Albert Einstein (1879–1955) – yes, the relativity chap – wrote to the US President Franklin D. Roosevelt (1882–1945) in 1939, warning that nuclear power was a jolly dangerous thing to be playing with, and would be of use to other nations. It was some years, though, before the Manhattan Project – which went on to develop the atom bomb – got under way, led by the physicist J. Robert Oppenheimer (1904–67).

On 16 July 1945, the first test of an atomic bomb – code-named Trinity – was carried out in New Mexico, creating energy equivalent to 20,000 tons of TNT.

Only certain nations admit to having nuclear weapons – the USA, Britain, Russia, China and France – but others, such as India and Israel, are thought to have them.

Oppenheimer worked as a government adviser in the States until 1954, but was then deemed a bad security risk because of previous contact with communists. This was during the paranoid days, when anyone showing the slightest tendencies towards the political left was branded a communist.

•

The gun More people are killed each year by small arms than any other weapon. Under the Second Amendment of the United States constitution, everybody is allowed to carry a weapon: 'A well-regulated militia being necessary to the security of a free state, the right of the people to keep and bear arms shall not be infringed.'

In the UK, as in many countries, firearms are not allowed to be carried except under licence and in strict circumstances (a farmer can carry a shotgun with a shotgun licence, but needs a Section One firearms certificate to use, say, a rifle or pistol. And that's more difficult to acquire).

Although it has been challenged from time to time by some legal eagles, there's still a provision in the US Constitution allowing citizens to carry firearms. That, coupled with a long history of the carrying of such weapons, means that it's hard to achieve gun control in the country.

It all began in the fourteenth century – guns, that is, not America's lack of gun control – when a thing called the firelock was developed. Basically, it was an iron tube closed at one end except for a tiny hole called a touch hole. That was where you put a heated wire through to ignite all the gunpowder inside, which sent the shot out at high speed. The barrel was set into a rounded piece of wood so it could be held under the arm.

This crude device – which sounds more dangerous to the user than to anybody he might point the thing at – later had a small depression called the flash pan, which held a charge of powder that was fired by something called a slow match: basically, a piece of cord soaked in a solution of potassium, which smouldered.

The matchlock came around the middle of the fifteenth century – a bit like the firelock, but the slow match was held in an S-shaped device, called a serpentine, which pivoted on top of the gun in such a way that, by pulling a trigger, you could bring the slow match into contact with the priming pan. Very clever, because it meant that the weapon could be operated with one hand.

The second decade of the sixteenth century saw the wheel lock. Pulling the trigger set the wheel going, and its hard rim scratched a lump of iron pyrites, sending sparks onto the powder in the pan; this also fired the weapon.

A thing called the 'snaphance' was invented early in the seventeenth century. This contained a piece of flint that was hit by a spring-loaded hammer when a trigger was pulled. This, too, produced pretty sparks for its deadly purpose.

Then came flintlocks, which modified and improved on the snaphance mechanism and became the main form of both shoulder and hand firearms from the late seventeenth to the mid-nineteenth centuries .

A revolution in small-arms manufacture and development came in the nineteenth century, with repeating rifles and smokeless powder, improved muzzle velocities and better ballistic qualities.

Reloading mechanisms were built into rifles that were operated either by the recoil or the pressure of the propellant gases. Once these were fed with belts of cartridges, we had the machine gun. Those that used magazines or large clips of ammunition were called automatic rifles.

The American M16 is an automatic rifle, although it's sometimes referred to as a machine gun. It holds twenty or thirty individual rounds in a magazine.

Light machine guns were used extensively by infantry in World War II, when firepower improved significantly.

One of the most talked-about guns these days is the Kalashnikov. This is an AK-47 assault rifle invented by Mikhail Timofeyevich Kalashnikov. This, and modifications of it, are used widely throughout the world, often being associated with terrorists and paramilitaries.

Food and Drink

Food is arguably the most widely eaten commodity on Planet Earth. Some of us just can't do without it. But whether you can call half the stuff we eat food is open to debate. Witness the mass-produced breakfast cereal, the instant 'crème' topping you get by just adding milk to some unspeakable concoction of cornflour and dubious chemicals.

But taste is a matter of taste, and we've looked at a few Great Ideas in the world of food to whet your appetite.

•

Chocolate Cacao tree equals cocoa beans equals chocolate equals scrummy! Native

Americans had cultivated cocoa beans for a very long time – nobody knows how long.

Cocoa beans were first brought to Europe by Christopher Columbus in 1494, but he didn't realize their value.

While on his travels, the Spanish explorer Hernán Cortés conquered Mexico in 1519. Breaking for a quick cuppa mid-pillage, he

observed Aztecs consuming large quantities of a kind of chocolate drink known as chocolatl, and brought it back to Spain on his return in 1528. Spain managed to keep it a secret for a century. Well, wouldn't you? But the French learned of it and in 1657 a Frenchman opened a 'chocolate house' in London. During the latter half of the seventeenth century, chocolate houses sprang up all over London and were frequented by politicians, wits, gamblers and literati.

Its popularity gradually spreading throughout Europe, it wasn't until 1847 that Fry and Sons of Bristol produced the first eating chocolate. This was a dark chocolate, and it was almost thirty years before the Swiss introduced the world's first milk chocolate – by adding powdered milk to the pressed cocoa bean – in 1875. Of little nutritional value, chocolate is a good energy source and a moderate source of iron; milk chocolate provides about two-thirds as much iron as dark chocolate.

But forget the nutrition and the fact that the

sugars rot your teeth and the fat makes you fat –
we think chocolate has to be nominated as one of
the all-time Great Ideas.

·

Pasta Italians eat tons of the stuff! As well as
in Italy, pasta constitutes a large part of the
national diets in China, Indonesia, Japan,
Vietnam, and – come to think of it – Britain. The
earliest references to pasta come from Sicily
during the period of Arab rule, but it is Marco
Polo who is popularly believed to have brought
it from China to Europe in the fourteenth
century.

Classic Italian pasta is made only from
semolina – it being the white starchy endosperm
of durum wheat – though, today, soft wheat is
often added. And, nowadays, pasta can also be
made using rice, buckwheat, mung-bean starch
or wholemeal wheat flour.

To prepare pasta dough, the flour is kneaded

with water. Often other ingredients are added to give different flavours and interesting colours. Egg yolk is used to produce a golden-yellow pasta, tomato paste for a red pasta, squid ink for a black pasta and spinach for a green pasta. A variety of shapes and cylinders are produced by rolling out the dough and cutting it into the desired shapes, or forcing it through a pasta machine to produce solid or hollow cylinders. It is partly dried in hot air, then dried some more, but more slowly. The pasta shapes or cylinders will then be either partly or completely dried. Dried pasta will keep for a considerable time without any loss of quality, whereas fresh pasta – which contains more water – keeps for only a week or so. However, fresh pasta can be frozen for later use.

Pasta is a very versatile food product. Commonly boiled and served with a sauce, it can be stuffed with a variety of other ingredients – meat, cheese or vegetables – and boiled or baked.

There are many varieties of pasta with names, such as spaghetti; vermicelli; fettuccini; linguini; tagliatelle. Lasagne and lasagnette are sheets of pasta. There are ribbon shapes and spiral shapes, coils and butterflies. Gnocchi or 'lumps' are shaped pasta dumplings and are used to garnish soups or served as a savoury dish with a cheese sauce. Potato gnocchi are pasta dumplings made from potato flour.

Macaroni, a short hollow tube of pasta can be used in savoury or sweet dishes. Other tube pastas include zitoni, fovantini and maccaroncelli. They can be straight, spiralled or sharply bent into an 'elbow', and penne are hollow, nib-shaped tubes. Cannelloni are long, wide tubes, normally stuffed with meat or spinach and baked in a sauce.

Pasta for soups can be ground, granulated or shredded (farfals), small lengths of vermicelli, or shaped like small stars, rings, shells, rice grains, letters of the alphabet, animals and all sorts of shapes to keep you amused at mealtimes.

Square envelopes of pasta stuffed with minced meat, cheese, vegetables or fish are known as ravioli; agnelloto is cut into a half-moon shape; cappelletti are hat-shaped. Of central European Jewish origin are Kreplach, pasta envelopes that have minced meat fillings and are cooked in and served with soup.

•

Bread Why should this be such a Great Idea? Well, bread can be served with just about everything.

Makes you wonder how it came about, though, doesn't it? It's a pretty unlikely thing to discover by accident. But that can be said of many things. Perhaps some ground grain and water were being mixed for some sort of basic, if rather pasty, meal and someone noticed that, when it was left by the fire, it rose, having probably attracted some natural airborne yeasts, and smelled rather appetizing. Perhaps one day it was left too close to the fire for too long and … who knows?

Whatever happened, every culture has developed recipes and methods for breadmaking of differing types, resulting in a very broad range. Bread flour can be made from grinding wheat (the grain most commonly used), rye, barley, corn, rice, potatoes or soya beans. There is the traditionally shaped loaf, but many more shapes, such as rolls, brioches, cobs, plaits and baps.

Wheat and rye flours are the only flours that produce gluten (elastic protein), which helps make raised loaves. Bread made from flour that contains the whole of the grain is of a denser texture because the bran and wheatgerm weaken the gluten.

The action of the yeast on sugars in the flour actually produces ethanol, which is the alcohol you get in booze! However, it gets vaporized during baking. The first bread, it is thought, was probably made from acorns or beechnuts. They would be crushed, mixed with water and left to heat, either naturally or artificially, so the grain became a sort of cake.

The Egyptians knew about bread baking before the twentieth century BC.

Today, we have commercial production, which makes for some less delicious alternatives such as sliced white bread. Even named brands, known for their quality, pale alongside hunky, chunky stuff ripped off a loaf. One of the worst things that can have happened to bread must be the Chorleywood bread method, which uses intense mechanical mixing of the dough to replace the first fermentation stage. Then fat and sugar are added.

•

Beer Beer is an alcoholic drink, made by the fermentation of solutions derived from cereals and other starchy grains. Most beer is made from malted barley and flavoured with hops.

It's also very tasty and refreshing, and it's a pity that it's become so much associated with heavy drinking and loutish behaviour.

In reality, the British have had such an anally retentive attitude to the wonderful amber liquid that some people tend to use it for just that: getting drunk and doing things they

(occasionally) then feel they have to apologize for. Connoisseurs see it in a totally different light – well, maybe not totally, because they do like to feel the effects, but different, anyway. The fact is that there are some wonderful brews around, if you know where to look. In the UK, the Campaign for Real Ale (CAMRA) has publications and websites to guide the would-be beer aficionado, and other countries no doubt have their own troops of dedicated enthusiasts who see it as their mission in life to preserve all that is good about beer.

In Japan (sake), China (samshu) and Korea (suk), rice is used to make beer. In Africa, millet, sorghum and other seeds are used. The Russians use fermented rye bread to brew kvass.

Osiris, the Egyptian god of agriculture, taught us to brew beer, or so it is said. The Egyptians of old buried barley pots for germination and they then used wild yeasts to ferment the mash malt.

We're accustomed to a bitter beer, of course, and the bitterness is imparted by hops – thought to have been first added to beer in the seventh century BCE. Beer was brewed in Northern Europe in the early Christian era, and, except for in Muslim countries, nowadays people can enjoy a glass or two (or three) of that wonderful brown nectar just about anywhere in the world.

•

Fish and chips Still together after all these years! Who'd have thought that the humble potato would team up with a piece of haddock or cod and become one of the most beloved dishes ever known?

Fish and chips were probably the first ever takeaway and are lumped among all the others in the fast-food industry – up there with hamburgers, kebabs, scooped ice cream – fried chicken and number 49 with extra house fries.

But, before the days of the takeaway, a fish-and-chip shop would be called a chippy. They weren't fast food or takeaway food: they were fish and chips.

Odd what you can do with semantics.

•

Other things that are bad for you Why are we saying things that are bad for you are a Great Idea? Well, it's one of life's ironies that you just love the things that can eventually kill you, whether it's chocolate, cream, beer, Bombay mix (full of good things but a calorific bombshell), cakes, sweets and other gooey stuff.

Chocolate we've dealt with elsewhere, as we

have beer. Cream makes up about 4 per cent of milk (4.8 per cent if it's milk from the Channel Islands). And, of course, it's rich in fat. And fat makes you fat. Single cream contains 18 per cent fat, and whipping cream 34 per cent. Double cream has a massive 48 per cent fat – but that's not the worst. Top of the list is clotted cream, usually from Devon or Cornwall, and it is 55 per cent fat.

Chips (*see* **Fish and chips**) are, of course, potato (full of starch) fried in fat. And fat makes you fat. The humble potato is actually a native of the Andes of Peru, but is found in all temperate countries these days, brought to Europe around the middle of the sixteenth century by Spanish explorers.

About 18 per cent of your average potato is starch – $(C_6H_{10}O_5)x$, but you always wanted to know that – and 78 per cent of it is water. At least that doesn't make you fat. And you do get about 2.2 per cent protein, and some vitamins, including the extremely healthy vitamin C.

Cakes are, of course, scrummy, especially fresh-cream ones (naughty but nice), and therefore Bad For You, as, of course, are all refined foods. Take sugar, for instance. It's reputed to be good for your teeth – if you chew the cane. Refine it to the white stuff you put in tea or add to cooking and it does just the opposite: rots your teeth. It also loses the vitamins and minerals it had in its natural state. (You could draw a stark comparison with cocaine here: the raw coca leaf was habitually chewed by native Peruvians, giving them a mild euphoria that was harmless and even helped them to work; now it's been refined into a highly dangerous drug. Not a Great Idea.)

As for the rest, well, just look along the supermarket shelves at all the ready-made desserts – all will taste nice, but then you check the ingredients and realize they're basically a load of starch with sweeteners, several chemical colours and flavours added.

Other Ideas

Most collections of facts have one: a 'miscellaneous' section. In here we have put together a few more Great Ideas we couldn't find suitable categories for.

•

The cross-reference
See **Circular referencing**

Wallpaper Some of the most tasteless room design imaginable is all the fault of this decorative paper used to cover interior walls. It was used as a joke in the seventies on the satire programme that launched Rowan Atkinson, *Not The Nine O'Clock News*, where the news studio was decorated in the most hideous wallpaper.

Wallpaper was developed as an inexpensive (read 'cheap', in many cases) alternative to tapestry, cloth, leather hangings or wood panelling. The history and manufacture of wallpaper have depended on the changing styles in textile design and the development of printing processes.

The study of wallpaper may not be everyone's idea of an interesting diversion, but read on: it has a fascinating history.

Wallpaper had come into use in Europe and China by the beginning of the sixteenth century. In France, in 1599, a guild of paperhangers was established. English stationers – already printers of box-lining papers – started printing rolls of the stuff towards the end of the seventeenth century.

In those days, most papers were block-printed in a repeat pattern and, in some cases, embellished with additional hand-colouring. By dusting powdered wool over a design printed or drawn with a sticky substance, an imitation cut-velvet wallpaper was achieved. These 'flock' wallpapers were soon highly sought after. Probably even more desirable were the wallpapers that actually came from China. These were painted or block-printed, hand-coloured papers that formed continuous scenes in the manner of a mural. Many examples have been carefully preserved on the walls of eighteenth- and early nineteenth-century houses in England and America.

English inventions, such as machine printing with engraved cylinders and continuous rolls of paper, greatly increased wallpaper production in the nineteenth century. Soon, with wallpaper meeting a wider demand and growing cheaper, the quality of design declined.

In reaction to this, William Morris (1834–96) – the English writer, poet, designer and socialist reformer, who, in an increasingly industrialized age, urged a return to medieval traditions of design, craftsmanship and community, and who was the prime figure in the formation of the Arts and Crafts Movement – began to produce better designs based on medieval motifs. However, the design of mass-produced wallpapers did not improve until after World War II, when new printing processes developed.

Since then, wallpapers with washable surfaces, pre-pasted and pre-trimmed for easier application, have made wallpaper, along with vinyl and fabric, an even more popular wall covering.

Wallpaper has an electronic form now, of course, as anyone with a computer will tell you. Your 'desktop' has a background pattern on which the program icons sit. And, yes, it's called wallpaper.

•

The Universal Declaration of Human Rights What could be a Greater Idea than human rights? This declaration was drawn up in 1948 – although to look at the world today, you'd think such a document had never been thought of.

There are thirty articles in the Declaration –

adopted by the General Assembly of the United Nations – governing such things as cultural, political, economic and social rights, including the right to life and liberty, freedom from arbitrary arrest, freedom of movement and residence, ownership of property, thought, conscience, religion, a standard of living adequate for health and wellbeing, and a few other good things.

Why are so many people starving, in prison arbitrarily, homeless, persecuted for having the wrong religion (or no religion at all), being deprived of their lives (be it by the gun, the bomb or lethal injections in prison cells)?

Still, the European Convention on Human rights – adopted in 1950 – contains most of the provisions in the Declaration, and was incorporated into UK law in October 2000 (having been incorporated into Scottish law in May 2000).

It means that a UK citizen can now pursue these rights through British courts instead of having to go through a whole nightmare of Euro-bureaucracy.

The tardiness of the British government to incorporate the articles wasn't the only example of procrastination, however. Oh, no. They signed the convention in 1950, but British citizens had to wait until 1966 before they could even go through the European Court of Human Rights.

•

Wales For whatever other reasons Wales is a Great Idea, it obviously falls into that category for broadcasters. It's odd how many times, in radio discussions of a small country or an island off a big country or an area of ocean or desert, you hear someone say, 'In an area the size of Wales …'

Call this a flippant observation, but we think they're using Wales as a mere convenience because they're too idle to find some other little parcel of land to make a comparison with, and we're making out a case to go before the Commission for Racial Equality. (Only joking.)

Actually, Wales is OK. What's more, it has lots of picturesque scenery and sheep and hills and valleys and sheep and beaches and sheep – and it has beautiful Cardigan Bay. In Cardigan Bay there are all kinds of sea life. As you'd expect – it's the sea.

Among this cornucopia of marine life are dolphins – huge dolphins. Dolphins the size of whales.

•

Universal language 'Sometimes I start a sentence in English y termino en español.' We don't know if anyone ever said that, but it's one of those standard jokes you hear to illustrate one point or another – in this case that there are so many languages that many people have to speak more than one in order to be understood by all their friends.

Going some way to reverse the Babel effect (Jehovah scattered them, with all their separate languages, all over the planet, remember) has been universal language, which is a natural or artificially constructed language, used to help people who do not speak the same language to communicate with each other.

Throughout human history – usually as a result of conquest and colonialism – various natural languages have been used as universal tongues. Often nations have been forced to abandon their own languages in favour of those of their new rulers, or have gradually assimilated the conqueror's language. In other cases – as with the Normans in England – it is the conqueror who has, over a period of time, adopted the language of the people they have conquered.

Sometimes, a nation that borders another of greater political, commercial or cultural importance will adopt that nation's language, albeit as an addition to, rather than replacement of, its own.

In the eighteenth and nineteenth centuries, it was the French tongue that was the most widely used universal language. For most of the twentieth century and now into the twenty-first, English has become the most prominent. However, in the past, it was Latin that came nearest of all native languages to becoming a truly universal tongue.

Communication through a universal means has also been attempted through using pidgin or *lingua franca*; also, by the use of existing languages in a simplified form. Such a language was Basic English, devised between 1925 and 1930. Proving in the end to be difficult to write while clearly preserving the meaning (because of the complexities of the English language and its grammar), it consisted of 850 words covering everyday needs, 400 general nouns, 200 picturable objects, 100 general qualities, 50 opposites and 100 operations.

Attempts to use existing languages as universal languages has often failed, owing to people's inability or unwillingness to learn them, more often than not because of nationalistic prejudices.

As a direct result of this, various attempts have been made to develop artificial universal languages. These have been based on natural languages, but simplifying spelling and grammar.

Johann Martin Schleyer – a German bishop – devised Volapük in 1880. Dr Ludwik L. Zamenhof – a Polish doctor – invented Esperanto in 1887. Both these artificial languages were based on Latin, German and the Romance languages. Unfortunately, in the case of Volapük, learning the language proved very difficult and so it never really caught on. Esperanto has been much more successful and is the most widely used artificial language today. It is often to be heard at international conferences, while several newspapers and magazines are published in the language, not to mention a large body of translated literature. Even the Bible and the

Koran have been fully translated into Esperanto. However, despite all this, Esperanto – quite unfairly in our opinion – does not have official status as an international language.

In 1951, the International Auxiliary Language Association created its Interlingua language by deriving from English and the Romance languages, and standardizing vocabulary based on the main Western European languages. Its use has mostly been in international scientific and technological journals, and has eliminated the need for costly multiple translations.

W. Ashby and R. Clark invented and pioneered a language with a 1,000-word vocabulary – Glosa – in 1981, deriving it from Greek and Latin roots.

•

Morse code This system of communication that's sure to make you dotty enough to dash for the whisky bottle was invented by one

Sam (that's . . . . – – –) Morse. Actually, it was Samuel Finley Breese Morse (1791–1872).

In the early 1830s, Morse – who was born in Charlestown (now part of Boston) in Massachusetts – began experimenting with electrical devices and completed his apparatus for electromagnetic telegraph in 1836. Morse code was born, enabling dotty messages to be dashed off by nimble-fingered telegraphers, who must have thought it was little short of a miracle. Imagine, sending words along a wire.

In 1843, Congress asked Morse to construct an experimental line between Washington, DC, and Baltimore in Maryland. And, on 24 May 1844, the first message, 'What hath God wrought!', was sent. What, indeed!

In the age of e-mails, fax machines, telephones and satellite technology, Morse code was used for distress signals at sea until 1999, when it was replaced by the Global Maritime Distress and Safety System, which uses both satellite and terrestrial radio communication.

What we'd really like to know is how Morse code represents a dash or a dot. Could be a bit confusing, that.

•

Circular referencing
See **The cross-reference**

Sun cream These days we're all afraid of the ozone layer – or, rather, the lack of it in places. So sun cream is a must, now that we all know about skin cancer and what can cause it.

Sun cream works by blocking out ultraviolet radiation, which has a wavelength of between 400 and 15 nanometres, or nm (you'll be fascinated to know that a nanometre is a millionth of a millimetre; or, for those who are still in the imperial days, 40 billionths of an inch). Sunburn is caused by UV radiation that's less than 310 nm.

It's a sobering thought, as you brush the sand off your face where it's stuck to the mixture of sun cream and sweat, that, if all the UV light from the sun were allowed to reach Earth, most life would cease. The ozone layer protects us from that – or did, until people started making holes in it with their use of chlorofluorocarbons, or CFCs, which were used in aerosol cans and as refrigerants. These chemicals contain chlorine and are broken down by sunlight, allowing the chlorine to react with the ozone molecules and destroy them. Hello, melanoma. Many countries have now banned CFCs.

Even so, keep that squeezy plastic bottle in your bag.

•

Money 'Money makes the world go around, the world go around…' or so that nifty little ditty from *Cabaret* goes. It's also said by some to be the root of all evil – although that's a misquote. It's the love of money that's the root of all evil, according to the saying.

It can certainly cause a lot of problems and most crimes can be blamed on the love – and lack – of money.

In days of old, people just bartered, and a sheep might have changed hands for a piece of equipment, or the chap who was an absolute whiz at making arrows might swap them for clothing made by the local seamstress.

Money, though, tends to be regarded as a keystone of modern economic life. It lubricates the process of trade and commerce. Basically, it's any medium of exchange that's widely accepted in payment for goods and services and in settlement of debts, and also serves as a standard of value for measuring the relative economic worth of different goods and services.

Apparently, first appearing around the sixth century BCE in Lydia, Asia Minor, coins rapidly proliferated throughout the world's more developed economies. On the orders of monarchs and aristocrats, cities and institutions began producing coins. These were stamped with identifying marks to testify to the coin's authenticity and grade its metallic value.

The Chinese qian, a round copper coin introduced in the fourth century BCE, remained a standard coin for 2,000 years.

Once established, the monetary system thus created remained essentially constant for millennia. In seventeenth-century Europe, one of the few enduring changes came about with the introduction of milled edges for coins. This change was introduced to deter clipping of coins, which had become fairly widespread because of the worth of the metal used to forge the coins.

Around the ninth century there came the introduction, in China, of paper money in the form of redeemable cash certificates issued for the Tang dynasty by private bankers. It wasn't until the sixteenth century that paper money came into use in the West and, even then, wasn't common until the eighteenth century. Paper money was issued as promissory notes by a bank against money deposits held at that bank. French colonial authorities in Canada used playing cards signed by the governor as a promise of payment from 1685, since shipment of money from France was slow.

Money can, of course, be created these days by the click of a mouse button or the press of a computer key. After all, it's only numbers.

Credit – a promise to pay in the future – has become an inescapable supplement to money today. Indeed, instruments of credit, rather than actual currency, are today used in most business transactions.

•

The Doctor Note the capital 'D'. This is the Doctor, who was such a Great Idea that there are no fewer than eight of him (his eighth incarnation is now going about with a face that uncannily resembles that of the British actor, Paul McGann).

The Doctor (only ignoramuses call him 'Doctor Who') is usually associated with endless corridors (being chased along), screaming female assistants (having to pacify), bright metal dustbins on wheels with sink plungers for arms (being threatened with extermination by) and an old-fashioned London police box that's bigger on the inside than on the outside (constantly repairing, occasionally by reversing the polarity of the neutron flow with the aid of his sonic screwdriver).

He's something of a bodysnatcher, and claims to be a Time Lord from the planet Gallifrey, although circumstantial evidence suggests that he may be a frustrated actor. He began life in 1963, bearing a remarkable likeness to William Hartnell. After a while, he decided he fancied a new face, so took that of Patrick Troughton. Took the body, too. Not satisfied with that (or perhaps bored with having to play the recorder), he decided to try Jon Pertwee's physiognomy for a while, before tiring of that and becoming a passable simulacrum of a witty, silken-voiced actor called Tom Baker – he of the long scarf. This one would appear to be the most popular of the Doctors.

However, there was to be another Baker, but not before there had been a Doctor who wore cricket gear and a Panama hat and looked like that chap from *All Creatures Great and Small* – you know the one: Tristan; yes, Peter Davison – all fresh-faced and 'effete', to quote his successor, the second Baker – no relation – a fleshly chap called Colin.

A famous spoon-player, with a penchant for sticking ferrets down his trousers, called Sylvester McCoy was the next likeness chosen by this chameleonic character. And then, with some help from the Americans, Paul McGann.

Confusingly, there may well be more of him. While parading around as Tristan, the Doctor was also spotted as Richard Hurndall pretending to be William Hartnell. Then a short time later, he was thought to be Maurice

Denham impersonating Richard Hurndall pretending to be William Hartnell, but that turned out to be another time traveller altogether! (You'll have to see the video!) And then there's Peter Cushing, Trevor Martin, Nicholas Briggs, David Banks, Michael Jayston, Rowan Atkinson, Richard E. Grant, Jim Broadbent, Hugh Grant, Joanna Lumley, Christopher Biggins …

They've all played the Doc at some time – on stage, celluloid or small screen.